ADULTHOOD

POCKET GUIDE
TO
ADULTHOOD

29 THINGS TO KNOW

BEFORE YOU HIT **30**

JASON BOYETT

[RELEVANTBOOKS]

TO AIMEE. THE CHANCE TO BECOME A GROWNUP WITH
YOU IS THE BEST GIFT YOU'VE EVER GIVEN ME.

Published by Relevant Books
A division of Relevant Media Group, Inc.
www.relevantbooks.com
www.relevantmediagroup.com

Design: Relevant Solutions
www.relevant-solutions.com
Cover design by Ben Pieratt
Interior design by Jeremy Kennedy

Relevant Books is a registered trademark of Relevant Media Group, Inc., and is registered in the
U.S. Patent and Trademark Office.

For information or bulk orders:
RELEVANT MEDIA GROUP, INC.
100 SOUTH LAKE DESTINY DR., STE 200
ORLANDO, FL 32810
407-660-1411

For booking information, visit *www.jasonboyett.com*.

Library of Congress Control Number: 2005931081
International Standard Book Number: 0-9763642-5-5

05 06 07 08 09 8 7 6 5 4 3 2 1

Printed in the United States of America

CONTENTS

INTRODUCTION

Because you picked up this book and are reading this introduction, it's not too much of a leap to assume you're approaching a certain Big Round Number. You have reached the notch on your timeline where decades matter, where numbers divisible by ten become really, really important—and really, really intimidating. You are approaching the age of thirty.

(Or, at least, you know someone who's nearing thirty, and this looks like a decent book for him or her. Or maybe you're just a little weird, and you get your jollies reading books that don't apply to your stage of life. In which case, that's cool, too. All paying customers are welcome.)

This being the first page of *Pocket Guide to Adulthood*, it's time to hook you—over the next few paragraphs—into this book and its subject matter. A good method for doing so would be to tell a real zinger of a story, something metaphorical and thought-provoking.

Or to introduce my own personal feelings about having turned thirty, an event which occurred in December of 2003, and which already seems way too long ago.

But the inspiring introduction is such a cliché, as is the bloggy personal anecdote. So, me? I'm going with shame. Gut-wrenching, emotional distress. The kind of stuff that'll grab you by the shoulders and shake you awake.

CONSIDER: In 1975, the thirty-year-old Gilda Radner was cast as the first regular on *Saturday Night Live*. (*At this point, pretty much everyone has done a lot more with his or her life than you have.*)

In 1993, Michael Jordan announced his (first) retirement from the NBA, at the age of thirty. At that point, Jordan had led the Chicago Bulls to three straight championships, and he'd personally loaded his bookcase with three straight Finals MVP awards and seven straight scoring titles. (*Yep, the dude retired at thirty. He wasn't just an overachiever. He was* finished *achieving.*)[1]

In 1804, Meriwether Lewis and William Clark began their journey up the Missouri River to find a water route across the uncharted West. Lewis was thirty. (*Seriously—are you even trying?*)

According to popular theory, the age of thirty is when you are supposed to have it all together. You become a grownup. All the muddle-headed flightiness of your twenties falls away, and the responsibility gene kicks in. It's serious business.

Are you prepared for it?

Probably not. None of us is. If thirty is the year when we suddenly become socially adept, financially stable and psychologically sound, then—if you're anything like me—we've got a long way to go. We're not ready to retire at the top of our game. We're not blazing new trails or on the verge of making history. We're not anywhere *close*. Nope, we're still looking for advice. Day-

---

1. Except for that part where he unretired and rejoined the Bulls at the end of the 1994-1995 season. And then announced his (second) retirement again in 1999. And then unretired again to play for the Washington Wizards in 2001. And then retired for good at the end of the 2002-2003 season. Allegedly.

to-day wisdom. Practical suggestions.

Fortunately for you, this book has all of that stuff, plus smoothie recipes! It's your handy little field guide to a respectable, secure, well-lived adult life. Take notes. Highlight. Scrawl in the margins. Browse.

And enjoy it. Because once you've finished reading, you're gonna have to get all responsible and adult-y and stuff. Good luck with that.

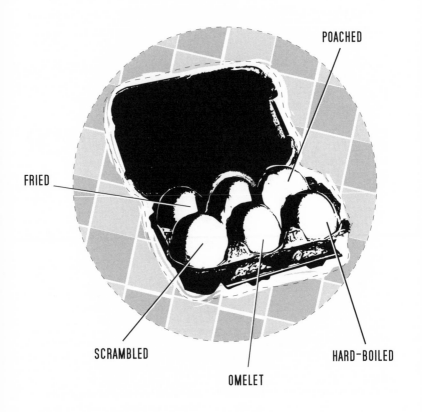

POACHED

FRIED

SCRAMBLED

OMELET

HARD-BOILED

CHAPTER ONE

HOW TO COOK EGGS A BUNCH OF DIFFERENT WAYS

Some facts about eggs: Your basic supermarket chicken egg contains nearly every nutrient known to be essential to humans. An average-sized egg tops out at about seventy calories. The egg is considered to be such an efficient source of protein that it's the standard by which the protein quality of other foods is measured.

Yep, eggs are good for you.[1]

Plus, they're yummy. That's why the ability to cook an egg is one of the most essential skills of adulthood. Sure, you could let others know you're at home in the kitchen by saying something like "Port du Salut makes a fine dessert cheese," but that's not nearly as cool as

1. In recent decades, the egg has suffered from some bad nutritional press, mainly a result of people getting all worked up over high cholesterol. This is not necessarily because eggs are an extremely high source of cholesterol, but because a breakfast of eggs usually also includes bacon and/or sausage and/or fatty biscuits and/or a whole lot of grease. It's cholesterol by association. But don't worry. You can eat two or three eggs per week without, say, clogging up an artery or something.

asking someone, "How do you like your eggs?" and then cooking them up to order.

Here's how to do it.

FRIED EGGS

Start off with really fresh eggs, which will hold the best shape (shape being a main concern in frying a good egg, because everyone knows a lopsided egg doesn't taste nearly as good as a lovely, concentrically yolked one).[2] Heat up a nonstick skillet. If you only have a regular skillet, grease it with a small amount of margarine or cooking oil, remembering that this will likely add fat or calories. When the skillet is hot enough to sizzle a drop of water, it's ready.

Break your eggs, one at a time, into the skillet. Some people prefer to break their eggs onto a saucer, then slip each egg off into the skillet from the saucer. This method is overly cautious and borderline anal-retentive. But to each his own.

Once the eggs hit the skillet, reduce heat to low. Cook the eggs slowly until the whites set and the yolks begin to thicken. For eggs sunny-side up, stop here. (Keep in mind that eggs prepared this way often are not fully cooked.)

For eggs over-easy or, my favorite, over-medium, you'll have to cook the other side by gently flipping it with a nonstick spatula. Doing this without breaking the yolk can be the trickiest part of the process. It takes practice, dedication, and nerves of steel. And a really wide spatula, if you can find one. If you have trouble with the egg flip, you can cook the top side by spooning a little water or melted butter onto the egg, then covering with a lid. Just don't tell anyone you had to resort to the sissy method.

Season as desired.

---

2. Grade AA eggs are the best for keeping their shape when you release them from their shells. They have thicker albumen (the white stuff) and firm yolks and are therefore ideal for frying. If you ask an egg what he wants to be when he grows up, he'll say, "Grade AA." At which point you'll want to seek psychological attention because, let's face it, you're asking questions of your eggs and, even worse, getting answers.

SCRAMBLED EGGS

Any fool can scramble an egg, right? Sure. But haven't we all had scrambled eggs that were dry, rubbery, and barely edible? There are scrambled eggs, and then there are *good* scrambled eggs. Here's how to make the latter.

First, break the eggs into a small bowl and use a fork or wire whisk to preblend the yolks and whites. Some choose to add a little milk at this point, for extra creamy eggs. Others may add a little water or melted butter. Some recommend adding salt at this stage, while others insist this makes the eggs rubbery and you shouldn't season food until it's on your plate. It's quite the controversy.

Preheat a nonstick skillet or saucepan at medium heat (or grease a regular skillet). Pour the egg mixture in, and then turn the heat down a little more. This is the secret to good scrambled eggs—low heat. If you allow the eggs to cook too fast or too much, you get the culinary equivalent of yellow packing peanuts. Using a wooden fork, spoon, or rubber spatula, stir all around the saucy eggs. Don't let the mixture sit long enough to crispify on the edge of the skillet.

Don't, don't, don't turn the heat up. Just keep on stirring. Once most—but not all—of the eggs move from a creamy state to a solid, turn off the heat (the eggs should still be a little shiny and very slightly underdone). Remove the skillet from the heat source, but keep scrambling until everything finishes cooking away from the heat. Serve immediately. The mistake many people make is to stir the eggs over heat until done. Then they turn off the burner, and the eggs continue to cook in the still-hot skillet. Silly people. Their eggs end up dry, overcooked, and chewy.

For kicks, melt cheese over your scrambled eggs. Or sprinkle on some chives. Or blanket them with a warm tortilla.

POACHED EGGS

Here's where you begin to enter the egg elite, as a well-poached egg is becoming a lost art. Start with fresh, refrigerator-cooled Grade AA eggs, which best allow the whites to gather neatly around the yolks.

Fill a medium-sized frying pan with a layer of water—two to three inches is ideal. Heat the pan to boiling, then reduce the heat as low as possible while keeping the water at a simmer. Expert's secret: Add a little vinegar and salt to the water at this point, which will help the eggs retain their shape. Break the eggs into a saucer, then dip the edge of the saucer into the water, sliding the eggs out to cook (you can probably pull off five eggs at a time, six if you're really heroic). Let 'em cook uncovered until the whites firm up. This takes between three and five minutes, depending on how solid you like your yolks.

Remove the eggs with a spatula or slotted spoon. Drain the eggs on a paper towel before serving. Try poached eggs on toast or a biscuit. For Eggs Benedict, combine them with an English muffin, ham or bacon, and hollandaise sauce. Bask in your superiority.

OMELET

For a two- or three-egg omelet, start by hand-blending the eggs in a separate bowl with a tablespoon of water. Experts recommend using a fork for this, so as not to over-blend. Add a little grated cheese to the mix.

The most important next step is to use the right-sized pan. Six to eight inches is ideal. If your skillet is too large, it won't hold the heat as well, resulting in a tough omelet. And a small skillet makes the omelet hard to fold.

Swirl a tablespoon of butter over the surface of the pan until it stops foaming. Then, turn up the heat and pour in the egg mixture.

Tilt and rock the pan so the eggs cover its entire surface. Leave everything in place for five full seconds, then push the cooked mixture to the center with a spatula. Tilt the pan and allow the uncooked part to flow back into its place at the bottom of the pan. Keep doing this until the omelet is slightly browned on the bottom and soft and moist in the center.

Add grated cheese and any other ingredients now by spooning them across the center of the omelet. Tilt the pan again and, with the spatula, fold one-third of the omelet over the center filling. Holding a serving plate in the other hand, tip the omelet onto the plate; the final fold will occur as it rolls onto the plate. Remember, as with scrambled eggs, the omelet will continue to "cook itself" due to its internal heat, so serve immediately.

HARD-COOKED (HARD-BOILED) EGGS

The easiest egg-cooking option. Place your eggs in a saucepan and cover with cold water (enough to cover the eggs by at least one inch). Rapidly bring the water to a boil, then cover the pan and remove from heat. Let stand. After fifteen minutes or so, cool the eggs down by first draining the hot water and then running cold water over them. Crack and eat. Decorate them for Easter. Make egg salad. Juggle. Balance them on one end during the vernal equinox. The possibilities are endless.

FINAL WORDS

A moderate serving of eggs is nutritious, delicious, and, when cooked properly, quite impressive. My dad can fry an egg over a mountain campfire in frigid weather using a rusty pocketknife, some squeeze butter and a Boy Scouts of America mess kit (circa 1964). If he can do that, then you can certainly cook a good egg in the modern convenience and comfort of your home. So get crackin'.

CHAPTER TWO

BEWARE THE CREDIT CARD DEBT MONKEY

If you're like most of us, you got hooked on credit cards in college. They were handing out free T-shirts or something to entice you to sign up. And that Discover Card tee? Was awesome.

Back then, you promised Mom and Dad that the card was just for emergencies. Unfortunately, you experienced emergencies on a regular basis, like needing pizza at two in the morning. Or needing to relax in Florida for spring break.

Then, before you knew it, you graduated with a whopping $18,000 credit debt distributed over three cards. You racked up nearly the same amount in student loans. And you were using the rad promotional T-shirt to clean the bathroom.

According to a 2003 analysis of student loan applicants by Nellie

Mae, a top provider of student loans, 96 percent of undergrads have at least one credit card. The average college student possesses six (!) credit cards and is more than $3,200 in debt; 10 percent of students are at least ten grand in debt. That's a whole freaking lot of emergencies.

The fallout is that a lot of young people leave college and enter the workplace with an evil, feces-throwing debt monkey clinging to their back, a financial burden that's well nigh impossible to shake. The under-thirty-five set is the least likely to pay their bills in full each month. Combine that with an average student loan obligation of $15,000 or so, and you've got an entire generation living on the financial edge for years to come.

It's not that we're idiots or lazy mooches or burdens to society. Most late-twentysomethings are hard-working and focused on their careers at this point. But saving for things like retirement or a future down payment on a home is hard enough as it is. And when debt is teetering over you like a cartoon anvil? *Imposíble.*

SO HERE'S A TIP: Credit cards can be dangerous. But you knew that already, right? Good. Let's move on to something more appropriate: How to get out of debt.

FIRST, THOUGH, THE CREDIT CARD CONUNDRUM

Credit cards aren't inherently bad. When used properly, they can be a valuable financial tool. They're convenient for making big purchases or for shopping online. They're helpful when renting a car or making a hotel reservation. And one of the best ways to establish a good credit history is by paying off a major credit card on time, every month.

But there's the rub: paying the entire balance month by month. That little "minimum payment" box is enticing, no? Book a cruise to the Yucatán, and all they want from you next month is $15! You can enjoy it now and keep your wallet full until you have the cash to pay for it. It all sounds wonderful, except for a little something called interest. Let's say your cruise costs $1,000 and your credit card interest rate is 15.9 percent (a pretty good rate). By making the minimum payments each month, it'll take you more than fifteen years to pay off the debt, by which time you'll have forked over nearly $1,400 *in interest alone*. That's more than the trip cost to begin with. Gulp.

And if you miss a payment along the way? That stain will be on your credit report for years to come—something creditors, insurance companies, and even employers can peek at in order to determine your financial responsibility. The moral? A couple of major credit card screwups can keep you from buying a house or getting a job.

You've heard it all before, of course. If you're going to use a credit card, you need to use it wisely. Find one that gives you cash-back bonuses or lets you collect points for airfare or other perks. Or at least find one that doesn't charge an annual fee.[1] Don't ever be late on payments. And if possible, use your credit card like a debit card and whip it out only when you can cover the expense.[2] That means you pay off your credit card bill in full at the end of each month.

That's worth saying again. Pay off your credit card bill every month.

HOW TO GET OUT OF DEBT

Of course, smart use of credit cards is often advice received too late. If you're already carrying a $5,000 balance, that's a secondary concern. The primary one? Your 18 percent interest rate,

---

1. Or, if you're already with a card that does charge a fee, take a stand. Customers who put a lot of purchases on their cards are held in high regard. The banks don't want to lose you. So call the customer service number and simply tell the operator you're not going to pay the annual fee. If they balk, tell them to cancel your account—you're gonna switch to a card without a fee (there are still plenty of those out there, and they know it). Most of the time this'll get them nervous enough to waive your fee for the year. Seriously, this works. You'll probably have to do it on an annual basis, but why not? How many five-minute phone calls can net you $50?
2. As long as you're pretending your credit card is a debit card, why not just get a debit card and use that instead? It has most of the perks and a lot fewer drawbacks.

compounded monthly. It's not going away by itself, so you'll have to take action. It's time to shake the debt monkey.

Suck it up and increase your payments. The minimum payment is what banks want you to pay—it lets them keep charging you interest. The longer you take to pay off the balance, the more money they make. So start forking over as much as you can each month. Cut your expenses. Sacrifice a luxury to the gods of debt management. Then take whatever money you save and apply it to your credit card balance. Dig deep and adjust your lifestyle.

Practice self-control. Don't put anything on your credit card that you're not going to pay off next month. Otherwise, you're countering your own attempt at debt reduction. If you can't discipline yourself to do this religiously, then get out the scissors. Cancel that sucker and use a debit card until you're debt-free. Otherwise, it's like complaining about your sunburn while lying naked on the beach. No one will feel sorry for you. But they *will* stare. After all, you're naked.

Beg. While you're working to pay down your debt, try to negotiate with your creditor for a lower interest rate. Explain your situation to them, keeping in mind a couple of things creditors fear. They're afraid you might be tempted by another card company offering a lower rate, causing you to transfer your balance elsewhere and deprive them of all the juicy interest. Or number two, they're afraid you might declare bankruptcy as a last resort, leaving them open to a loss. As a result, many creditors will often go the extra mile in working with you. Never hurts to ask.

By the way, if you're successful in lowering your interest rate, that doesn't mean you can lower your payments accordingly. Keep paying the same amount. That way, the money that used to go toward interest can now be applied to the principle, which decreases the total debt load faster.

Borrow. This is the tricky part, because it requires some serious thought and occasionally can introduce negative consequences. Still, paying off your debt with borrowed money is worth considering. *Hey, wait a second,* you're thinking, *the best way to get out of debt is to get into more debt?* The answer is a) Possibly, and b) I don't like your tone.

HERE'S THE DEAL: Say you've got a $5,000 debt that's growing at an 18 percent interest rate. Very, very bad. Why not pay off the card by getting a loan at a lower interest rate? You'll still be in debt, but the interest will be much less painful. One option is to borrow from your 401(k). Most plans will let you borrow a certain amount, at a rate a couple of points above prime—which, most of the time, is way cheaper than 18 percent.[3] Do your research, though, as many plans limit your borrowing abilities to important stuff like medical bills, education, or a first home.

A better option is to borrow from friends or family, but approach this with extreme caution. The really loving ones may give you an interest-free loan, but don't expect it—this is money that could be earning interest if they weren't such suckers for your woe-is-me story. Instead, tell them you'll pay a point or two over the prime interest rate, whatever it is at the time.[4] If you take this route, make things official. Sign a written agreement, establish a payback and interest schedule, then stick to it—disagreements over money can ruin friendships and tear apart families. Don't let this happen. Be kiss-their-feet grateful and remain utterly resolute in paying off the loan.

---

3. Even better, the interest you pay on 401(k) loans eventually goes back into your own pocket—it goes into the borrower's account, not the lender's. But ... you'll have to repay this loan in five years or less, according to the rules. And should you switch jobs before paying it back, the loan must be repaid immediately or it will be considered a partial distribution of your funds. And since you're younger than fifty-nine-and-a-half, that distribution will be taxed a 10 percent early withdrawal penalty. There can be major drawbacks to this strategy, so think about it first.
4. The prime rate is the amount charged by banks to their customers with the best credit. It has been rising steadily since late 2004. As of this printing, it was around 6.5 percent.

DEBT CONSOLIDATION

Debt consolidation is another good option for paying cards off. Debt consolidators (also known as "credit counselors") are nonprofit agencies that help you negotiate with creditors to get your debt in line.[5] They go over your expenses and help you decide what you can afford to pay each month, and then they work with your creditors to merge unsecured debt (think credit cards or medical bills, but not mortgages or car loans) into a single payment. These nonprofits can often negotiate lowered interest rates on your behalf, which allows you to pay more toward the principle. Then, you write just one check to them each month, and they disburse it to your creditors. Who, at this point, are supposed to stop calling you.

Watch out, though, for consolidators who make promises they can't keep, like repairing your credit history or wiping it completely clean. Um ... you can't do that, at least not legally. There are no do-overs in the land of credit history. The only way a credit report can be altered is if you change your Social Security number—which is pretty much illegal. Back away.

If everything's on the up-and-up, though, debt consolidation may be a viable option. Look into it, but be careful.

FINAL WORDS

Credit cards are like dynamite. When used properly—in carefully controlled situations and for a specific purpose—they can be very helpful. But when handled recklessly, that little piece of hologrammed plastic can be deadly. Because so many people have failed to recognize the danger of uncontrolled credit card use, credit debt has become (and will continue to be) a major problem.

---

5. But not all debt consolidation agencies are nonprofits, and not all nonprofits are there just to help. Nonprofit status is just a way to organize a business. Some debt relief agencies aren't afraid to take advantage of your desperation by offering a quick fix. In short, they profit off your problems. Be cautious. Avoid agencies that require upfront fees or promote "payday" or title loans.

Understanding how to use your credit card properly is one of the most important things a grownup needs to know.

And if you've already discovered that danger firsthand and ended up burned, then getting out of debt is one of the most important things you need to do. It won't happen overnight. It requires tightening the belt and tailoring a budget (see chapter 19). It involves sacrifice and smart spending—whatever is necessary to help you make the biggest payments you can every month. It'll be a challenge, but you can do it. In fact, you *should* do it, and you should start now.

03

HOW TO SPEAK GOOD ...
ER, WELL

There's a saying in the British Isles: "Speak one way, and you'll be running the country. Speak another way, and you'll be cleaning it." Across the pond, speech patterns and usage are hugely important, calling attention to everything from education level to birthplace to social standing. Things aren't so cut-and-dried in the United States. In fact, our forty-third president—the one "running the country"— has been known to publicly mangle a sentence or two. Still, there is a right and wrong way to speak, and there are people in our society to whom this stuff is very important. They're called English teachers, and they can be harsh. They'll judge you for the way you talk.

Maybe you personally don't care when someone says "lie-berry" instead of *library*, but others do. You could find yourself in a job interview conducted by a former English teacher. You could be making a marketing presentation to a group of grammar-obsessed executives. You could fall into a brief, random conversation with someone for whom proper speaking is a virtue. In any of these situations, you don't want to immediately call attention to your lack of linguistic polish.

That's why achieving adult status means being able to speak clearly and semi-articulately, which requires a basic adherence to the rules of grammar. Unfortunately, grammar is boring, and most of us tuned it out in ninth grade. We didn't care then, nor do we care now. Some of you have stopped reading already.

Losers.

For those of you who are still around, however, we've identified two of our most frequently confused grammar scenarios—*lay* versus *lie* and *good* versus *well*—and will hereby attempt to shed light on the differences between them with style and clarity and delightful humor. Or, at the least, muddled rambling and sarcasm. We'll play it by ear.

LAY VS. LIE

In its most basic form, the rule is this: "Lie" is an intransitive verb, meaning it does not take a direct object—it's something you do to yourself. Therefore, you're going to lie down.

> *I have eaten a bad taco, so I think I should* lie *down.*

It follows that "lay" is a transitive verb—it's something you do to someone or something else. As a result, "lay" is followed by a direct object.

Because the bad taco tastes like feet,
you should lay *it down and walk away.* (object: it)

I'm gonna lay *down my burdens,*
down by the riverside. (object: burdens)

Easy, right? Yes, it might seem so, until you consider the past tense, which is where most of us get screwed. The past tense of "lie"? You got it: "lay."

I lie *down today. Yesterday, because of the taco,*
I lay *down.*

The past tense of "lay"—the transitive verb, the one you do to something else—is "laid":

I lay *down the bad taco today.*
Yesterday, I laid *it down.*

And just for kicks, let's look at the past participles. First, the past participle conjugation of the verb "lie" is "lain":

By this time tomorrow, I will have lain *down*
for twenty-four hours, because of that stupid freaking taco.

The past participle conjugation of "lay" is "laid":

By next Tuesday, he will have laid *down thirty bad tacos*
in a seven-day period, which must be some kind of record.

It's all becoming clear now, right? Let's continue.

GOOD VS. WELL

Scenario: You meet an old friend from high school. He smiles, sizes you up, wonders whether he's more successful than you, calculates which one of you has put on more weight (note to self: lay off the tacos), then asks, "How've you been doing?"

Most common response? "I'm doing good."

Nope. Wrong answer. You're not doing *good*—you're doing *well*. Confusing the two is so prevalent in our society that hardly anybody notices it anymore. In fact, some dictionaries have begun classifying the mistake as informal usage. But we know better than to accept that, because there is something to be said for being an above-average speaker of English.

"Good" is an adjective. It modifies nouns and pronouns:

> *Your tattooist did a good job on that winged demon.*
> ("Good" modifies "job.")

> *A winged demon is a good choice for a neck tattoo.*
> ("Good" modifies "choice.")

"Well," on the other hand, is an adverb. It's used to answer the question "How?" as a modifier of verbs, adjectives, and other adverbs:

> *How did your mom do during the tattooing process?*
> *She did well.*
> ("Well" modifies the verb "did.")

> *I'll say this for your mom—she wears a winged demon tattoo well.*
> ("Well" modifies "wears.")

So, athletes don't "play good," and singers don't "sing good." They play well and sing well. That's easy enough. The trouble starts when we start linking verbs and subject complements, especially when we talk about how we feel or how we are. "Feel," like forms of "to be," is a linking verb. It connects the subject with a subject complement. For instance, in the sentence "You are dumb," the subject (you) is linked to the complement (dumb) by the linking verb (are).

Unfortunately, "good" and "well" are both often used as subject complements. Therefore, "I am good" is just as correct as "I am well." Same goes for "I feel good" and "I feel well."

Yeah, grammar pretty much sucks. But let's keep moving.

Here's the difference. In a subject complement situation, "well" should refer to health or the body:

> *I don't feel well in my stomach,*
> *especially after seeing that tattoo.*

> *I am well, except for this debilitating nausea.*

Meanwhile, "good" is used to describe your mental/emotional state or your character:

> *I thought I'd feel good after punching that obnoxious clown*
> *right in the squeaky nose, but I was wrong.*

> *Michael Jackson may be a nut job and a generally bad person,*
> *but I am good.*

TO SUMMARIZE: Good speakers of English speak well, and feel good about doing so. Though the copious amounts of grammar in this chapter may have given you a headache—preventing you from feeling well—the information was presented well enough to give you a good grasp of the difference between "good" and "well."

And that's all well and good.

FINAL WORDS

Of course, the real question you're asking, despite the eloquent defense of proper speaking at the beginning of the lesson, is who really cares? And honestly, that's a valid point. Because unless you're one of those strict but well-meaning grammar zealots, standing fast behind good sentence construction like it was the final stronghold between doilied tea parties and anarchic desolation, *lay* versus *lie* doesn't matter that much in the grand scheme of things. It ranks right up there with being able to name the ten highest mountains in the world or the shortest and tallest U.S. presidents.[1] Let's all admit it—it just feels more natural to say "I'm gonna go lay down" or "we're doing good," doesn't it? Even though technically wrong, the incorrect usage is so prevalent in our society it might as well be right.

Language is funny that way; it's entirely fluid. What's proper today might fall out of favor tomorrow, and vice versa. Consider *The Flintstones*, who, upon their debut in 1960, promised viewers "a gay old time" right there in the theme song. (Not that there's anything wrong with that.)

So lay down if you want, particularly if you don't feel good after a bad taco encounter. But while you are doing so, remember that the best way to get people to take you seriously and respect you is to sound intelligent when you speak to them. First impressions are important. Bad first impressions can be deadly. Don't fall prey to one just because you think grammar and vocabulary are for geeks. They are, of course, but in today's world, geeks are running the show.

---

1. In order: Everest, K2, Kangchenjunga, Lhotse, Makalu, Cho Oyu, Dhaulagiri, Manaslu, Nanga Parbat, and Annapurna, all of which are in the Himalayas. Abraham Lincoln was the tallest president, at six foot four. James Madison was the shortest at five foot four. And he weighed less than one hundred pounds, so I could probably have taken that shrimp down hard. In case anyone was wondering.

CHAPTER FOUR

FIRST DATES ARE HARD, EXCEPT IN HOLLYWOOD

You know the movie *Before Sunrise*? The 1995 film starring Ethan Hawke and French actress Julie Delpy? The movie everyone in our generation absolutely loves because it has such great conversations and a wonderful love story about Jesse and Celine and how they meet on the train and spend a fabulously romantic up-all-night fourteen hours on the streets of Vienna in, like, the best date ever? And how they drink coffee and engage in witty wordplay and get their palms read and meet a street poet and kiss and then never see each other again? Never again, at least, until the sequel, *Before Sunset*, came out in 2004.

That's not real. That never happens. Raise your hand if you've ever had a whirlwind love connection on the streets of some twinkly European city. Raise it high. Nobody? Thought so.

The spontaneously enchanted date is a fixture of film and television, but it rarely happens in real life, especially if you don't look like Julie Delpy or Ethan Hawke. But we looooove the fantasy date. We dream about meeting that perfect someone, of the electric shiver when our hands accidentally touch, or the flicker of interest we hope we just saw in an eyelash flutter or a half-smile across the room. We want movie love, TV romance.

We're into the roses and massages and candles and, um, camera crews of crap like *The Bachelor* and celebrity TV weddings. Then we go out on a real-life blind date with Stacy, cousin of Lydia from work. Unfortunately, Stacy hates dogs and you have a dog, and she's vegetarian and you took her to a steakhouse, and she's got this piece of lettuce plastered against one of her teeth the entire meal, and, sorry, it just doesn't work out. Date's over. You go home alone.

Where's the predawn kiss on the streets of Vienna? Where's the Vermont bed-and-breakfast? Where are the street poets?

ANSWER: They're in Hollywood, apparently. But in real-world dating—the kind experienced by living, breathing, three-dimensional people, like you and me—this stuff doesn't happen. First dates are never as easy as they appear in the movies. Nor are they as complicated. (Ever been in one of those TV situations where you mistakenly book two dates for one evening? Ever thought you could actually pull it off? No?)

So, to make sure your thirty-year-old expectations are accurate and not hopelessly lost in Hollywood fairy-tale land, here are the three major Hollywood dating archetypes to delete from your brain.

1) THE DATE OF GREAT EXPENSE

Friends ended in 2004 but is still in our collective consciousness because its reruns air every single day on every single channel in the known universe. I like the 1997 episode where Monica meets this guy, Pete, at the diner where she's temporarily working. He convinces her to go out for dinner with him. "I know this great Italian place," Pete says. Sure, says Monica. So this guy Pete—who turns out to be an Internet billionaire—flies her to Italy. For dinner. First date. Someone she just met. Happens all the time.

Or perhaps you can relate to a slightly less preposterous scenario: the pricey night-on-the-town date. Since a vast number of television shows are set in New York City, let's use that environment as an example. How many dates on TV involve some combination of the following? Dinner at the Four Seasons or its equivalent in midtown Manhattan (expect to cough up close to $200 for drinks, a meal, taxes, and tip). Follow it with attendance at some swanky event. A charity ball? That's another $150 a head. Knicks tickets? Upward of $60 a seat. Add a cab to the mix, and you're on your way to needing a calculator.

Now let's be honest here. Short of the night you propose marriage, is it necessary to spend that much on a date, even if, at this point, you have the cash flow to even consider it? (Which is no guarantee, even at thirty.) It's not gonna happen that often. Good thing, too, for those of us who are not Internet billionaires.

And if you're expecting some guy (or girl) to come around flashing enough currency to do the stuff listed above, well, stop. Stop with the outsized expectations. If you do encounter it, be cautious. What's Mr. Moneypants trying to prove? Is he generous or just showing off? Is he trying to snow you on the first date by spending fistloads of money? Does he want you to be impressed by him or his wallet?

ONE LAST TIP: If a guy wants to take you to dinner in Rome, and you live in Akron, Ohio, he's trying too hard. Way too hard. Score one for overcompensation.

2) THE HIGHLY INAPPROPRIATE VENUE

I don't care how awesome Death Cab for Cutie is, Seth, a concert at The Bait Shop is not the best place for a first date. Keeping with the movie theme, I reference a memorable scene in Cameron Crowe's 1992 film, *Singles*. You're almost thirty and fairly hip, so it should still be on your radar. Campbell Scott and Kyra Sedgwick first meet each other at a live concert. Standing fifteen feet from a noisy, stomping grunge band, the two attempt the awkward, "Come here often?" introductory conversation. And that's fairly difficult while shouting at each other above the power chords and budding tinnitus.[1] They eventually get together, then break up, then get together again—but nothing happens at all until they meet each other again in a quieter, more intimate setting.

So, live music venues—not ideal for a first date. Same goes for a dance club, unless the two of you have both acknowledged a fondness for salsa dancing or the Electric Slide or whatever. Don't expect much in the way of conversation, though. Ditto for movies. Two hours in a dark room with booming audio and no talking is not the best place to get to know a person. So why select it for a first date?

3) THE QUEST FOR SEX

Here's where it gets fun. I refer you to the generally sleazy world of television dating shows, in which the plot pretty much revolves around skeezy twentysomethings trying to get laid. For instance, syndicated shows like *Blind Date* and *elimiDATE*, where a typical episode starts in a bar and, three minutes later, ends in a public hot tub. The women are usually surgically enhanced and desperate. The guys are all ripped and horny. You get the feeling the girls are thinking "If I act like a whore, he'll like me." And the guys are

---

1. **tin·ni·tus:** noun: a ringing or buzzing in the ears. Defined in the movie as "club disease."

thinking, "She's acting like a whore. I like her." Then they do body shots. This is followed by tasteful filler like grinding set to music, groping set to music, skimpy attire being revealed, skimpy attire being removed.

Don't forget these are *blind* dates. These are people who didn't know each other prior to the show. Not that this stops them from, say, licking ice cream off each other's abdomens within an hour. But not your typical date. Not even for Julie Delpy.

Keep in mind that all this is captured by cameramen and willfully released to a national audience. *Not* the best picture of dating. Don't expect body shots and public nudity on your first date. Don't expect to always be asked up for, um, a "cup of coffee" at the end of the date. Don't expect to be followed around by a camera crew, either.

FINAL WORDS

So when contemplating a first date with someone, steer clear of Hollywood's dating clichés. Don't spend too much, don't choose the wrong venue, and don't anticipate ending up in the sack. Don't count on anything being easy.

But enough with the negatives. How can you make a first date successful? Be friendly and courteous. Be on time. Choose the right activity (one that lets you get to know one another, and something you both enjoy). Go someplace affordable. Keep it relatively short. Plan on talking about yourself, but be prepared to ask a lot of questions about your date. Make eye contact. Find common ground. Be curious, warm, enthusiastic. Ask nonthreatening, open-ended questions. Keep the focus on the present rather than the past (old flames) or future (a potential relationship). Pay attention. Be real.

If none of those work, fire up the jet and head for Rome.

EXPERIENCE
WHAT TO KNOW
SELL YOURSELF
EDUCATION
REFERENCES
OBJECTIVE

05

HOW TO CRAFT A SPECTACULARLY AWESOME RÉSUMÉ

In the axiom-rich world of marketing, it's often said that a client is looking for one of two things—a good feeling or a solution to a problem. It's the kind of cliché the workplace gurus toss around like a superball, bouncing it off any and every available surface.

But they're right, of course. Good feelings and practical solutions are what we're all after. Doesn't matter if we're conscious of it or not—we almost always consider a form of these criteria during each decision-making process, whether we're evaluating a university professor or hiring a babysitter.

The same can be said for those employers who are wading through stacks of résumés in hopes of finding someone who can solve their problem (filling a vacant or new position) and give them a good feeling (filling a vacant or new position with an employee who will not steal legal pads).

So keep that in mind during the next few moments. Take a deep breath, strap on your safety harness, and please keep your hands and feet inside the vehicle at all times—we're about to condense your entire life into a single letter-sized page. Maybe two pages, if you're lucky. It's called a résumé, and how to effectively write and prepare one is required knowledge.

WHAT IT IS

The word *résumé* is a French term that means "to summarize." And that's literally what it is—a summary of who you are, a synopsis of why you should be hired. For the purposes of this discussion, though, let's approach the résumé from a different angle. Not as a static list of achievements and experiences, but as an advertisement, a piece of salesmanship. It's a form of marketing. The subject? You.

WHAT IT NEEDS TO DO

A résumé needs to get attention—the good kind of attention— and hold it long enough for a prospective employer to pick up the phone and give you a call.

Here's how it works. Manager Jim is given a mandate from high up the corporate ladder. "Hire someone to fill the position, Jim," he is told by his boss. So Jim puts an ad in the paper or posts a listing on a Web site: "Position available. Excellent blah, blah, blah. Looking for blah, blah, blah. Competitive blah. Send résumé to Jim."

Four days later, Jim finds himself peering over a stack of 243 résumés burning a hole in his coffee-stained desktop. The corporate suits are still pushing him to make a hire, so he's anxiously shuffling through the pile. Jim is in scanning mode. He's not reading anything in-depth. At most, he gives each résumé about twenty seconds—ten seconds less than an average television ad—to make an impression.

Not all impressions are positive. For instance, Jim gets one résumé that is typeset in a flowery, unreadable script. He squints at it for maybe three seconds before crumpling it up in frustration. Another grabs his attention because it's printed on fluorescent orange paper. The color makes him dizzy. He refuses to read a word.

Then he gets to one that gives him pause, and this time it's in a good way. The page itself is clean and organized, but it does more than just inform him—it excites. It spurs him to action. He picks up the phone. He asks for an interview.

That's the purpose of a well-crafted résumé: not to get you a job, but to secure an interview. It's your foot in the door. Problem is, there are usually lots of other people hoping to jam their Kenneth Coles through the exact same door at the exact same time. That's why you must do something to stand apart, to get invited in. You need a résumé that will highlight your skills, sand over your splinters, and boost you toward the job you've always wanted. Or at least the mailroom *near* the job you've always wanted. (After all, everyone has to start somewhere. Just ask Jim.)

EVEN THOUGH IT FEELS STUPID, WRITE AN OBJECTIVE

Start with your name and contact information (address, phone number, email address). Center this part, put your name in all caps, and make it three or four type sizes larger than the body of the document.

After this comes the "Objective" section of your résumé—the short sentence that states "this is why I'm applying." It should be specifically targeted for the job in question and needs to be quick and to-the-point: *"A desktop operator position for a book publisher"* or *"An elementary-level teaching position for the Dallas Independent School District."*

Some have argued that the objective statement is archaic and a waste of space. Others disagree.[1] This is the place to grab the reader by the nose from the very beginning. How? By showing that you've researched the position or company and know what is being offered, and that you have a career direction and know precisely what you're looking for. In the example above, two-thirds of the résumés Jim receives will be of the shotgun variety, from people who send a résumé to every job listing they see. When Jim comes upon yours—customized via the objective statement for the specific job he's looking to fill—it'll give him pause. He'll know you're not just casting your seed to the wind.

SNEAK IN THE GOOD STUFF

There are several different styles of résumés, each of which have strengths and shortcomings. For our purposes, we're going to discuss the most basic style—the chronological résumé—simply because most employers prefer it.[2] A chronological résumé lists your most recent employment and experiences first, then works backward.

After the objective statement, the rest of your résumé must answer a simple question: What makes you the right person for the job? For most of us, it's a combination of experience, talents/ skills, and education. The first two of these will be covered in the "Experience" section, a line-by-line history of your working life, packaged as advertising. Every word has meaning.

This is where you sell yourself. Don't think for a second you can get away with just listing your employer, position, and period of employment. Nothing's more boring, unless you were once a covert

1. The objective statement is worthwhile as long as it's specific to the job offered. Generalized blanket statements like "A challenging position that will allow me to utilize my gifts and talents to contribute to the company while offering opportunities for growth and advancement" are worthless. The only purpose they serve is to indicate you didn't take the time to customize your résumé or that you have no idea what you want to do.
2. Other useful styles include the *functional résumé* (which focuses more on certain skill sets than detailed experience and is useful for people changing fields or with a wide variety of loosely related experience) and the *curriculum vitae* (which is primarily used when entering a teaching or science position, wherein things like publications and honors are considered in detail). Obviously, a C.V. can be much longer than your average one- or two-pager.

government assassin. (In fact, you might think long and hard about including that on your résumé anyway.) Instead, punch up your employment list with details. Describe what your job involved, what problems you solved, and what projects you handled. Summarize your responsibilities while focusing on the qualities that will make you most attractive to the person reading them.

SOME EXAMPLES:

Project Coordinator, Midwest Printing, St. Louis, MO
(2003-2005) Worked closely with dozens of customers in conjunction with sales representatives and prepress/printing staff to take projects from initial development stage to final printed and bound piece. Included conceptual brainstorming, production scheduling, and detailed proofreading for wide variety of projects—including product catalogs, regional direct mail campaigns, and consumer magazines.

(Since "project coordinator" is a vague term, this explains the particulars of your job—while also revealing your familiarity with large-scale projects, your organizational skills, your proofreading experience, and your frequent client contact. Regardless of the job, each of these skills is attractive to almost any employer.)

Grant Writer, Bailey-Templeton University, Kansas City, MO
(2001-2003) Duties included researching funding opportunities, writing grant applications, and developing grant proposals for a midsize private university. Worked closely with nonprofit and charitable boards and planned/hosted a number of social fundraising events. Was successful in procuring nearly $3.5 million for capital improvements and scholarships over the course of fourteen months.

(It's one thing to say you were a "grant writer." It's quite another to say you were instrumental in adding a cool three mil to the university's coffers. Even though that's not an abnormally high amount for a well-established university, it sure *sounds* impressive, particularly to the uninformed. Notice how this summary also touches on interpersonal, leadership, and organizational skills by way of the sentence on fundraising events.)

The most important thing to remember is to use descriptive writing to make your past jobs seem dynamic and productive. Perhaps your last work was as an administrative assistant, and your main responsibilities were entering data, photocopying, and answering phones. There's nothing wrong with that, but such a description is about as exciting as boiled potatoes. Spice it up a little. First, think of a problem you helped solve. Then, depict that problem-solving process with inspiring language.

Let's say you answered phones for a travel agency during the summer. It was a menial job, but you were good at it. So good, in fact, that the boss noticed your customer skills and asked you to develop a list of phone etiquette tips for the rest of the agency's employees. So instead of just saying you "answered phones," you can say you "helped research, devise, and implement new customer contact procedures." You may have held an entry-level position, but your job description delivers much more than that. You show yourself to be a problem-solver. That combination of critical thinking and assertiveness is something all employers are looking for.[3]

TAILOR YOUR EXPERIENCES

If you're applying for a job as research assistant for a medical supply company, there's no need to list your eighth grade paper route. Nor will the PR firm care that you were a lifeguard at the municipal pool during the summer after junior year (though CPR certification might be worth mentioning).

---

3. Please, please, please don't misunderstand here. I'm not saying to exaggerate or embellish your job experience. Lying on a résumé is all kinds of wrong, and it'll eventually catch up to you. What I'm recommending is the use of active word choice and selective descriptions to make your duties—however conventional—seem impressive. A successful résumé showcases your skills through the strategic use of detail.

The point is, you don't need to list every job you've ever had. The most recent two or three absolutely need to be there, but after that, list only the ones that are impressive or applicable. Ask yourself this question before summarizing your duties: Was any aspect of this job relevant to the position currently being offered? If so, line-list the job and show how it applies. Let's consider the municipal lifeguard applicant. If she's applying for a job at a PR firm, the only reason she might want to list her summer lifeguarding experience is if part of that experience shared common ground with the desired position. Here's how that might look:

Lifeguard, Clifton Marks Municipal Pool, St. Louis, MO (2000)
Duties included enforcement of rules and regulations and overseeing safety of all swimmers. In addition, worked closely with pool manager and local media in promoting "Fun in the Sun" Summer Swim Camp for underprivileged youth—wrote press releases, oversaw radio ad/PSA production, and served as media contact.

Notice how she listed her broad-spectrum lifeguarding duties first, then expanded on the more important advertising/marketing aspects. A similar applicant looking for a nursing position after graduation should focus on the medical aspects of her lifeguarding job.

Lifeguard, Clifton Marks Municipal Pool, St. Louis, MO (2000)
Duties included enforcement of rules and regulations and overseeing safety of all swimmers. Received and have maintained lifeguard, first aid and CPR certifications. Assisted in demonstrating first aid and CPR techniques for new employee orientation/training and attended additional Red Cross lifeguarding classes on Automated External Defibrillation (AED) and Oxygen Administration.

Whoever is reading your résumé doesn't want to know every single thing you did in your job history. But they do want to know about the things that might make you ideal for the job. Don't make them hunt for the pearls in your résumé—highlight those qualities.

MISCELLANEOUS TIPS

Education. While all experts agree that the details of your education are necessary, there is some discussion as to whether it should appear before or after your work history. My advice would be to put it first if it meets one of the following criteria: If your major was directly related to the position offered, or if you attended a prestigious school (e.g. Stanford, Vanderbilt, Rice, Duke, or any Ivy League university). If it'll be an attention-grabber, put it first. If you graduated with an unrelated degree from a ho-hum institution, put it toward the end of the résumé. List the name of the school, your GPA (only if it was a 3.4 or better), the degree(s) you received, and your major and minor. If you haven't yet graduated, include only the most up-to-date info.[4]

Additional Information. This is the potpourri category, the place to include any information that doesn't readily fit into work history or education but could be instrumental in selling yourself. For instance, you might want to list civic awards or charitable work. If you can speak another language or are a published author (no, blogs don't count), list it here. List fluency or experience with relevant computer programs or any leadership positions that might prove helpful. Almost anything is appropriate here *as long as it pertains to the job being sought.*[5]

---

4. If you attended college but never graduated, don't make a big deal of it. Instead, write something like "Attended Smith University, 1997-2000, majoring in French Literature with a minor in Business." The subtle difference between "attending" a university versus actually graduating from one may be lost on the speed-scanning employer.

5. The "Additional Information" category is an ideal place to cover the touchy subject of race or ethnicity—if, that is, it can be used as an advantage. An often unmentioned aspect of the job application process is that employers are sometimes pressured to give special consideration to minority applicants. Unfortunately, employers can't always tell minority status from a name (and it's not exactly kosher to write "Steve Wilson, Black Man" at the top of your résumé). Your best bet is to drop the hint by listing affiliations to which you belong: *Vice President, University of Notre Dame Black Students Association (2003);* or *Member, Society of Hispanic Professional Engineers (SHPE).*

Format. Keep it simple. Keep it organized and aesthetically pleasing. Don't use goofy fonts. Do use bold fonts, a larger type size, or capitalization to highlight the most important items, but keep whatever methods you use consistent throughout the résumé. Absolute parallelism is necessary—if you put periods at the end of a subhead, then make sure you do so for every subhead. If your previous job title appears in bold, then make sure all titles are bold. Print the résumé on a nice white or cream paper stock, and don't be afraid of too much white space in the margins or between sections—this makes it easier to read.

Usage. Since your résumé needs to be action-oriented, leave out as many articles (a, an, the) and personal pronouns (I, me) as possible. Spell out numbers up through nine, but use numerical form for ten and above. Proofread. Then proofread again. Then have someone else proofread it. A mistake in a résumé can cost you a job, so no typos.

Length. While you'll occasionally read that the basic chronological résumé should always be one page, that's not life-or-death advice—it's definitely up for discussion. I'd rather present a two-page résumé than trim something important just because I'm running out of room. The length doesn't matter; appropriate, enticing content *does*.

Accuracy. Do not put anything on your résumé that you can't back up. It's important to impress your reader, but not important enough to risk your integrity on propaganda. Keep in mind, though, that it is okay to highlight your best features and downplay your deficiencies. Have you ever seen an ad for an SUV that mentioned its sucky gas mileage? No—instead you're told about cargo capacity, safety features, and the powerful engine. In the same way, your résumé is an ad for *you*. Don't stretch the truth, but don't be so honest that you call attention to a monstrous negative. Use creative language to turn that negative into a positive: inexperience becomes "fresh perspective," a lack of skills becomes "willing to learn," and so on.

References. At the end of your résumé, include the phrase "References available upon request." While it's important to supply applicable references to your would-be employers, it's not always smart to list them on the résumé itself. By submitting them separately, you're free to tailor your reference list to the job being offered. You'll usually be asked for these following the first or second successful interview. Include three people with whom you've worked in the recent past—and, no, relatives don't count. These references should be able to vouch for your personality, honesty, work habits, etc. Some employers actually contact the people on your list, so make sure you get your references' permission before handing over their names and info. And the most important consideration of all: Make sure your references like you and will speak well of you. Good references can be the icing on the cake, but a bad reference can negate everything.

FINAL WORDS

Halle Berry may be naturally beautiful, but drape her in a bulky jumpsuit and a ski mask, and that beauty's hard to see. She might as well be Cafeteria Lady Marge. Same goes for your résumé—make sure you sell yourself by making your strong points easy to see. Don't make your prospective employer search for them.

And don't be afraid to seek help in writing your résumé. We've covered some basic principles and ideas, but there's a lot more to it than the few pages you've just read. Plenty of résumé-writing guides are available in print or online, as are countless formatting and design examples. Take advantage of these. Look at as many samples as you can to get a good idea of what works. Then, allow yourself enough time to do it right—a good résumé can't be typed up in fifteen minutes. So there you have it. Now go find a job.

06

BEING ALL WEIRD ABOUT FOOD SAFETY IS A PRETTY GOOD IDEA

So here's a life-affirming piece of data: The Centers for Disease Control (CDC) estimates that seventy-six million cases of foodborne illness occur every year in the United States. Yep, food poisoning. Most of these cases are mild—victims might suffer from flu-like symptoms for a day or two, including stomach cramps, diarrhea, and fever. But some cases go further. An estimated 325,000 people require hospital visits each year. And up to 5,000 die annually from some form of food poisoning.[1]

To put that into perspective, compare that with something else

1. "Foodborne Infections," Centers for Disease Control and Prevention Online, Division of Bacterial and Mycotic Diseases: Disease Information, updated January 10, 2005 (*www.cdc.gov/ ncidod/dbmd/diseaseinfo/foodborneinfections_g.htm*).

most Americans have experienced to one degree or another—automobile accidents. According to the Bureau of Transportation Statistics, there were an estimated 6.3 million car wrecks in the United States in 2003.[2] That's fewer than one-tenth the number of foodborne illnesses. Granted, more people are injured from vehicular accidents every year (almost three million), but those kinds of wrecks aren't nearly as common as the culinary ones.

Foodborne illnesses occur when bacteria are given a chance to thrive in a warm, moist environment. It follows that certain foods, then, provide a great starting point, especially foods high in protein and moisture. Milk and dairy products, eggs, meat, poultry, fish, and anything containing any combination of these products are highly susceptible to bacterial growth. These are all healthy foods and good for you to eat, but mishandling them can lead to trouble.

To top it off, when food poisoning does occur, it's hard to pinpoint exactly what has caused it and when. Sometimes symptoms show up immediately. Other times, they can take several days to slog through your system, making it difficult to identify the culprit. So how do you prevent foodborne illness? Just like you try to prevent injury in a car wreck—by making safety a habitual part of your driving. You pay attention to the road and to other drivers. You strap on a safety belt. You keep your tires inflated. Food safety is the same way. By making a habit of it, you can keep a bad batch of chicken salad from causing a gastrointestinal wreck. Here are the food safety tips and procedures you ought to put into practice.

KEEP HOT FOOD HOT

In eighth grade Home Economics, many of us were told it's a good idea to let leftover foods cool down before stashing them in the fridge in order to keep the refrigerator from having to expend

2. "National Transportation Statistics by Mode: 2004," Bureau of Transportation Statistics (*www.bts.gov/publications/national_transportation_statistics/2004/html/table_02_03.html*).

42

so much energy on the actual refrigeration side of things. Little did we know that the Home Ec teacher was trying to kill us. She was aged and married, so it should have been quite clear: old wives' tale. Not a good idea. Leaving hot food on the counter until it cools to room temperature is like wearing a Clay Aiken shirt to a biker rally—it's an invitation for something unfortunate to happen.

Here are two numbers you should remember: 40°F and 140°F. The space between those temperatures is the happy zone for bacterial growth. At these temps, bacteria multiply like nympho bunnies. Therefore, you need to keep your hot foods above the safe temperature of 140°F, which is too warm for bacteria to do much more than sit around complaining about the sweltering heat. That means eating your pizza within two hours of delivery. Or refrigerating uneaten hamburger patties within two hours of grilling (one hour if you're outside on a summer day). The same goes for any other leftovers—find a place for them in the fridge as soon as you clear the table.

KEEP COLD FOOD COLD

Same concept, different direction. This will make you feel good inside: Raw ground beef and poultry products, including eggs, often already contain illness-causing bacteria like E. coli or salmonella, respectively. Yes, friends, *they come that way*, even while on the shelf at the neighborhood grocery store. Not to worry, though—these latent bacteria are destroyed when you cook foods thoroughly. And when frozen or refrigerated, the microbes are practically paralyzed.

That's why meat and poultry should stay in the fridge until you're ready to cook. That's also why great care should be taken on picnics, camping trips, or when grilling out to make sure your cooler stays cool. Fill it with ice or frozen gel packs. Keep it out of direct sunlight. Keep the lid closed, and avoid leaving lunchmeats, potato salads, pasta salads, meat, chicken, and other perishables out of the cooler for very long. If you fail in this regard, bite the bullet and toss out the offending food. Better to do without another chicken salad sandwich than to spend the next day, um, pursuing another agenda.

AVOID CROSS-CONTAMINATION

As stated above, before meat and poultry are cooked (and the microorganisms in them killed), they could be harboring illicit illness-causing bacteria. That's why it's important to keep them from cross-contaminating other foods or utensils. This is probably the area of food safety wherein people are the most careless, so pay attention.

The best thing to do when it comes to raw meat or poultry is to *separate*. Keep them away from other foods—in your grocery cart, in your refrigerator, on your kitchen counter. Don't slice raw chicken on a cutting board, and then plop down a head of lettuce right where the chicken was. Unless you washed the cutting board with soap and warm water between foods, you've just contaminated your lettuce. Shame.

Same goes for serving platters and utensils. Don't take a plate full of raw sirloins out to the grill, fire things up, and then put the cooked steaks back on the same juicy plate. Leftover bacteria on the platter could contaminate the safely cooked food. Another rule: Never taste or reuse the marinate in which you've already soaked raw meat, poultry, or seafood unless you boil it first. (If you intend to use it later as a sauce, just keep some of it separate from the raw food.) You'll also want to pay close attention to the arrangement of food in your freezer and refrigerator. There's nothing worse than raw chicken juice dripping onto your apple pie. Actually, there are some things worse—like worldwide apocalypse via rogue nanobots—but that's another chapter, another book.

THAW SAFELY

Here's another example of motherly advice gone wrong. Don't thaw frozen food in the sink, on the counter, out on the sidewalk, or anywhere other than the refrigerator or the microwave. Back to the 40°F/140°F rule—you don't want raw foods sitting around in the danger zone, which is exactly what happens if you thaw a slab of frozen ground beef at room temperature. Don't do it, even if Mom used to thaw the Thanksgiving turkey in the bathtub. It's just plain wrong.

The safest way to thaw is to let the frozen food defrost slowly in the fridge. If you forget to plan far enough ahead to do this, it's okay to use the defrost setting on the microwave, as long as you cook the food immediately afterward.

KEEP STUFF CLEAN

This one's obvious, right? You'd think so. Most people are smart enough not to handle raw chicken and then, for instance, lick the poultry juice off their hands. But what you might not realize is that our hands have bacterial microbes on them all the time, even *before* handling raw foods—and for that reason, it's just as easy for us to transfer bacteria to the chicken, where it can spring to life and start reproducing wildly (the bacteria, mind you, not the chicken ... though that would be interesting). So wash your hands with warm, soapy water both before and after handling raw meat, poultry, and seafood. Wash any utensils, including meat thermometers and grilling tools. Same goes for serving platters, cutting boards, and any other surfaces that come into contact with raw foods. Pay particular attention to your sink and kitchen counter where other foods are likely to be prepared.

FINAL WORDS

Food safety is all about risk management. By handling food properly, you can significantly decrease your risk of exposure to foodborne illness. While there's no reason to become obsessive or paranoid about it—washing your hand fifty times a day because you just *know* they're crawling with salmonella—there's also no reason *not* to make the above tips part of your daily kitchen or outdoor grilling routine.

A delicious meal is one of life's great joys. That joy decreases exponentially when it results in vomiting.

07

HOW TO CHANGE A FLAT TIRE LIKE A REAL, LIVE MECHANIC

If you drive at all, and you aspire to adulthood, you need to know how to change a flat tire. Otherwise, you'll find yourself stuck by the side of the road some day, either waiting for AAA to arrive or worrying that some deranged scarface with a hook for a hand will stop and offer to help. Both scenarios can easily ruin your afternoon.

So here's your guide to hook-handed psycho prevention, step by step.

1) PLAN AHEAD

Before you take off for any sort of lengthy drive, always check for a couple of tire-related items. First, make sure you have a spare.

In cars, you'll generally find the spare under the floor of the trunk. Most trucks and SUVs stow the spare beneath the chassis at the rear. Whether it's a full-size spare or one of those temporary high-pressure "self-destruct-after-fifty-miles" donuts, make sure the tire is both accessible and fully inflated.

Next, confirm the location of both the jack and a tire tool. These are usually found in the same place as the spare. Often, the tire tool that comes with the car is small and wussy and hard to manage. That's no good. Get yourself to an auto supply store and purchase a brawny, burly jack—one of those drop-forged cross-shaped ones. Not only are they comforting in their religious symbolism, but they give you much better leverage on sticky lug nuts. More on that later.

2) PULL OVER SAFELY

When a tire gets punctured by road debris or suddenly blows out while you're driving, you'll know it—the way your car handles will noticeably diminish. You'll experience a little unsteadiness at the steering wheel or a pulling to one side. Don't panic and don't overcorrect. Instead, slowly apply pressure to the brake while steering to the side of the road.

At this point, you'll need to find a good place to jack up the car. It needs to be as far away from traffic as possible, especially at night when oncoming cars will have a difficult time seeing you crouched at the side of the road. It also needs to be a firm, level surface—you don't want to use a jack on a hill or incline.

Anyway, stop at the first good spot you find along a straight section of road (curves are dangerous). If you have to, it's okay to drive a short distance on a flat tire, as long as you do it very slowly, realizing that the farther you drive, the greater the risk of damaging the tire or the wheel itself. When you come to a stop, shift the car into park (or, for a manual transmission, reverse) and apply the parking brake. Turn on your emergency flashers. If it's dark, you might also want to turn on one of the vehicle's interior lights to help you see better.

3) SPARE, JACK, WHEEL COVERS

Find your spare tire, your jack, and your lug wrench, and arrange them within reach. Usually, the jack handle will double as the lug wrench, but if you're using a true lug remover (the testosterone-satisfying cross-shaped one), that won't matter.

There are several types of jacks. Yours may be a bumper jack that fits into a slot beneath the bumper. Others are screw-type scissors jacks that should be placed under the vehicle axle or suspension. Your owner's manual will contain instructions for operating the jack. Often, a decal near the spare tire will have the same info.

If you can't figure out how to use the jack, you'll need to locate an incredibly strong person who can lift up more than one thousand pounds and hold it steadily for, say, ten minutes. If such a hero is unavailable—just your luck—call roadside assistance. Jacking up a car is reasonably safe, but it can be tricky. If you aren't certain how it's supposed to work, don't risk it. Get help.

Your next step before actually putting the jack to use is to expose the lug nuts, which sounds really dirty but isn't. The lug nuts are behind the wheel cover or hubcap, which will need to be removed. Pry it loose using the flat end of the lug wrench or jack handle. Once the hubcap comes off, don't let it roll away. That can be embarrassing.

4) LOOSEN THE LUG NUTS

Before jacking up the car, you'll need to first begin loosening the lug nuts. Otherwise, the wheel will just spin on you. Find the end of the wrench that fits and place it snugly over any of the lug nuts. Turn counterclockwise, using the crossbar of the wrench to gain leverage. This can be awkward, as lug nuts often are so tight they don't budge on the first attempt. Don't worry, though—we're prepared for this scenario. Here's what you do: Steady the wrench with one hand and step down hard on the other end. If that doesn't work, steady yourself on the car and climb up onto the wrench. Put your full weight on the left-hand side of the wrench (yet another reason to get the big cross-wrench—this is much more difficult with the jack-handle version) and give it a good bounce. But be careful.[1]

Once you get the nut going, loosen it one or two full turns while the wheel is still on the ground. It should be loose enough that you can turn it the rest of the way by hand, which you'll do after the car is jacked up. Lather, rinse, repeat.

5) MEET JACK

To remove the wheel, you'll need at least a half-inch or so of ground clearance. This, of course, is where the jack comes in handy. First, insert the handle into the socket on the jack. To begin lifting the vehicle, you'll either turn the handle or pump it like scissors (again, check your owner's manual to see what type of jack you have). Raise the jack until it barely touches the car, then position it according to the directions in your manual. Each car has a certain place near each wheel designed for safe jack contact. It's usually less than a foot behind the front tire or a foot ahead of the back tire.

Once your jack is positioned correctly, give it a few good cranks. Lift the vehicle so that the tire has enough room to spin; then lift it a little more. After all, you'll need to fit a full-capacity inflated tire in its place. For good measure, crank the jack a couple more times.

1. And for Pete's sake, don't try this *after* you've jacked up the car.

6) OFF WITH THE OLD, ON WITH THE NEW

Hopefully, the lug nuts are still on the old wheel.[2] Turn them by hand until they completely loosen, then remove them. Don't misplace them—a good idea is to rest them in the basin of the nearby hubcap.

If you have gloves, this would be a fine time to put them on, as tires can be dirtier than a political campaign. Grab the old wheel on either side and pull it straight off. At this point, extra cautious tire-changers will sometimes place the old flat tire and wheel under the side of the car. That way, should the jack fail, the car won't fall to the ground, damaging its underside and squashing you like an ant on the street during a steamroller parade.

Moving on. Put the old tire aside and install the new one by lining up the spare's center holes with the threaded shafts on the wheel base. Depending on how high you've jacked the car, you may need to raise it another notch or two to have room for the new tire. Tighten the lug nuts as much as possible—stopping just short of fully tight—while the wheel is raised off the ground. Then lower the jack.

Now it's time to tighten the nuts the rest of the way. To make sure the wheel is securely balanced, work in a star-shaped pattern. Give a full turn to the topmost nut. Skip the next one, then give another full turn to next lug nut. Carry on in this manner through three or four tightening stages, until every nut is secure and flush against the wheel.

FINAL WORDS

Congratulations. You're done. Lower the jack according to the instructions in your owner's manual. Once the weight is removed, the jack will likely topple over. After this occurs, keep bringing it

---

2. Honestly, it's excruciating not to make this whole chapter into some sort of testicular joke. I'm practically boiling in my own snark.

down until the jack is fully closed. Then, all that's left is to clean up after yourself. Put the wheel cover or hubcap back on. Stow the damaged tire, jack, and tire tool back in your vehicle. Wipe your brow, pat yourself on the back, climb back in, and buckle up. Revel in your newfound mechanical skill. Then carefully ease into traffic.

NOTE: If you replaced your flat tire with a small, temporary, space-saver tire, please remember that it's only intended to allow you to drive to the nearest service station. It's not designed to take you a long distance, nor is it designed to go in excess of 50 mph. Drive carefully to the next facility and have your flat repaired by professionals. They'll fix it and put the repaired or new tire on for you.

And if they have any difficulties performing this task, you'll be right there to give advice.

CHAPTER EIGHT

MARRIAGE IS NOT NECESSARILY A ROWDY SEX ROMP, AND OTHER MISCONCEPTIONS

In recent years, marriage has been a permanent fixture in the usually fleeting world of the television news ticker. There was the whole Federal Marriage Amendment flap. You had all the healthy, kind discussions about gay marriage. Celebrity weddings and divorces are a weekly occurrence. Every other reality show these days involves people getting married on TV or meeting their future spouse on TV or switching their spouse with someone else's spouse on TV.

And despite popular anxiety about cohabiting couples or commitment-phobic twentysomethings, people in the twenty-five to thirty-four age bracket still see marriage as the model living arrangement. According to the U.S. Census Bureau, 50 percent of men and 57 percent of women this age are married and living with their spouse.[1]

That doesn't mean the "model living arrangement" is always so pleasant, especially for a generation whose parents set the standard for divorce back in the '70s and '80s. We've all heard the statistics. First marriages have a failure rate of more than 40 percent.[2] Second marriages end in divorce 60 percent of the time. Many young people experiment with "starter marriages," noncommittal practice runs that hardly count.[3]

The basic question is why? And despite culture warriors' attempts, the answer is probably not something that can be blamed on gay marriage or unfaithful celebrities. While there are plenty of reasons young marriages flatline, the biggest culprits seem to be the participants themselves and our own misplaced expectations. Despite our parents' failures, we think we know what marriage is. After all, we've seen it work ... on TV. As kids, it was the 11:00 p.m. slow dance of Cliff and Claire Huxtable. Maybe today it's Homer and Marge Simpson, still together after all these years. But the reality rarely matches our high-def dream. And when that happens, we scrap the covenant. Wasn't meant to be. Irreconcilable differences.

The differences aren't the problem, though; our irreconcilable *expectations* are. Before we say "I do," perhaps we should look a little

1. Data from 2000 U.S. Census Bureau projections: National Vital Statistics Reports at the Centers for Disease Control and Prevention.
2. The commonly cited statistic is that 50 percent of marriages end in divorce. This number is usually arrived at by comparing the number of marriages and divorces in a given year—which usually occur at a 2:1 clip, thus the conclusion of a 50 percent divorce rate. However, that fails to consider marriages in total (especially people who are already married and have been for a long time). A better statistic is this: Of first marriages, 43 percent end in separation or divorce within fifteen years. Source: Matthew Bramlett and William Mosher. "First Marriage Dissolution, Divorce, and Remarriage: United States," Advance Data from Vital and Health Statistics: No. 323 (Hyattsville, MD: National Center for Health Statistics) p. 21.
3. Check out Pamela Paul's intriguing *The Starter Marriage and the Future of Matrimony* (New York: Random House, 2003). In it, Paul—an editor for *American Demographics*—examines the growing phenomenon of twentysomethings who are getting married and divorcing within a few years before kids arrive. She calls this low-commitment first union a "starter marriage" and discusses its impact upon Generation X.

more closely at those expectations and, well, dump them out of the box. Here's what marriage isn't.

A CURE FOR LONELINESS

In a society where we're plugged in twenty-four hours a day, where "community" is more often used to describe the blogosphere than an actual neighborhood, people long to connect intimately with someone. Our culture puts great emphasis on hooking up, whether at a physical, emotional, or psychological level. Being alone is hard.

We see couples everywhere—in restaurants, on TV, on the subway or train or sidewalks on the way to work—and feel like something is missing from our un-coupled lives. Humans have an innate need to belong, and who better than a husband or wife to provide that acceptance and intimacy and comfort?

Best-case scenario, that's what a good marriage does. But we all know couples in warm, loving relationships who remain lonely. Why? After all, they've found a perfect mate, someone to possibly fulfill their need for intimacy. But that's a heavy load for one person to bear, which is why plenty of lonely single people become lonely married people. If your destination in marriage is to find someone who'll satisfy your need to belong, your next stop may be heartbreak.

AN ESCAPE FROM BOREDOM

In 1991, *U.S. News & World Report* reported that half of U.S. workers said the reason they had a job—aside from the necessity of earning a living—was to keep from being bored. In a separate survey, 25 percent of teenagers said they drink alcohol for the same reason.[4] Drug abuse experts almost always cite boredom as a leading excuse for experimenting with drugs. That's where all the talk about idle minds and the devil's workshop comes from—we do stuff simply because there's nothing else to do.

How many people get married for the same reason, because it's the next step after graduating college and getting a job and exploring the dating scene? Life gets dull, and it's easy to convince yourself that a serious relationship will make the day more bearable. Marriage is built-in happiness, right? Automatic entertainment. Regular conversation. At least you get someone to watch *Conan* with.

Unfortunately, this misses the true cause of boredom, which isn't necessarily an external lack of stimulus, but rather an internal one. You're not bored because you've seen every celeb-reality show on VH1 at least thirty times. You're bored because you can't come up with something better to do.

Getting married in order to generate a little excitement in your life is a terrible motivation. Why? Because once the merry-go-round stops—once the novelty wears out—you'll immediately start looking for the next ride.

A ROWDY SEX ROMP

As the old experiment goes, put a penny in a jar for every time you have sex during the first year of marriage. Then, beginning with your second year, take a penny out every time you do the horizontal two-step. Chances are, you'll still be pulling pennies a couple years later.

Does the lovin' stop after twelve months of wild newlywed monkeysex? Not by any means. But is every night a page out of the *Kama Sutra*? Nope. Guys, your wife doesn't want to be groped every time you climb in bed. And ladies? Keeping the romance alive is hard work for your husband. Sometimes we just want to watch *SportsCenter*.

Still, with communication and sensitivity, sex can (and should) remain a vital part of marriage. It's the ultimate bonding activity for a couple to share. But remember it's not the *only* activity. Don't expect marriage to be a fifty-year honeymoon of libido and lipstick.

MAKEOVER TIME

How often have you heard this? "He's not really interested in the stuff I like to do, but that'll change once we get married." Few marriages that launch from that pad end up happily ever after.

If there's anything you should know about marriage, it's this: Saying "I do" may change your legal relationship, but it doesn't change your character. An unhappy single person will be an unhappy married person. A thoughtless single person will be a thoughtless married person. An obnoxious single person will be an obnoxious married person. Don't enter a marriage expecting to remodel your husband or wife into someone else. You can't. People have baggage, stuff we've wheeled around since high school. It's been with us so long, few of us have the willpower to drop it before entering the wedding chapel. The flaws are a part of the package. They follow us right down the aisle, up the steps, on the honeymoon, and over the threshold.

Don't marry someone for who they might become. Marry them for who they are right now. Otherwise, they're likely to become nothing more than your ex.

AN EASY TRANSITION

There's a reason romantic movies end, rather than begin, with a wedding. It's because that's when the hard stuff starts. You have to unpack after the honeymoon. You have to write insincere thank-you notes for the tacky bathmats. You have to get used to sharing a closet and a sink with another person. The gap between singlehood and marriage is huge.

"I wasn't ready for all the changes," a married friend once told me about those first few months. "I could deal with moving into her place and giving up my furniture. But what surprised me was having to deal with her emotions. When you're dating, you always see her best face. Once you get married, you see everything."

Women don't have it any easier. Many secretly wince at the notion of placing their fate alongside that of another, worrying that the role of wife might eat into their individuality. Toss in holidays spent with another family and comparisons with Mom's cooking, and you've got explosive issues to deal with from the get-go.

There's no way around these adjustments. In order for the marriage to last more than a week or two, you'll have to find a way to cope. You won't be taken by surprise if you expect hiccups going in.

FINAL WORDS

Now, a disclaimer. We've been discussing what marriage is not, but here's what marriage *is*: Marriage is wonderful. There is no better way to make it through life than with a partner who loves you despite your morning breath and your bed hair. Marriage is deeply satisfying, incredibly fulfilling, and loads of fun. It softens the harsh edges of life. It brings joy and hope and laughter. It usually involves lots of sex.

But relationships are never easy, and marriage isn't something to rush into without thinking. When so many marriages are ending in divorce, it's clear that a lot of us are taking the plunge without knowing what's in the pool. Expectations aren't being met, and folks are climbing out hurt and disappointed.

Don't make that mistake. Look forward to the benefits, but expect the challenges, too. Know your potential mate. Temper your expectations with realism. Then, jump in with both feet. You're gonna like it.

09

CHAPTER NINE

HOW TO STOP WORRYING AND BE AN OPTIMIST

Pretend you're a good, hard-working employee, and upon arriving at work on Monday, you encounter your boss in the hallway. "Good morning," Mr. Bossman says. "I need to talk to you about something. Come by my office after you get settled in."

What's your first thought? A pessimist will automatically turn apprehensive, back-scanning the last few days to figure out what he might have done wrong. To the pessimist, everything is his fault. When something bad occurs—even something ambiguously bad, like a vague statement from a supervisor—he assumes the worst. He broods. His energy decreases. Taken to the extreme, his health may suffer, and he may eventually become clinically depressed.

As for the optimist, her thought process after the Bossman encounter swings an entirely different direction: *He wants to tell*

me how good a job I did on the Daniels account, our optimist may think. *He's going to promote me. Maybe I'm getting a raise. Maybe I'm getting a bigger office.* The optimist doesn't automatically jump to the worst-case scenario, but assumes a more positive outcome. And when actual obstacles do arise? They're not such a big deal. Those challenges are simply extra hurdles in the race. The optimist may be surprised by the hurdle and stumble a little, but she picks herself up and starts running again.

The line between optimism and pessimism is fuzzy. Few of us are entirely one or the other; there are hardly any true Pollyannas in the world, just as there are few who can out-Ebenezer Scrooge. Most of us fall somewhere in between, and our response to a difficult situation can fluctuate from one side to the other depending on the week, the season of the year, the way we feel physically, and even how we started our day. You knew this was coming, but here's a tip as you roll toward adulthood: Optimism is better than pessimism.

"Hang on there, Captain Obvious," you're saying. "You can't just suddenly *make* yourself into an optimist. Some people are wired to think that way, right?"

Right. Some people do have naturally optimistic or pessimistic tendencies, though most of us are more inclined toward the negative. In fact, we might as well consider low-frequency pessimism to be normal. But that doesn't mean we can't escape it. Pessimism doesn't have to be permanent. You can get rid of it piece by piece, like stripping bark from a tree. It's a slow process, but it's necessary for a well-lived life.

LAYING THE SMACK ON PESSIMISM

In the 1991 bestseller *Learned Optimism*, psychologist and clinician Martin E.P. Seligman details the roles optimism and pessimism play in regard to quality of life. He believes who we are—and what we become—are deeply related to how we explain life's stumbling blocks to ourselves. He writes: "The defining characteristic of pessimists is that they tend to believe bad events will last a long time, will undermine everything they do, and are their own fault. The optimists, who are confronted with the same hard knocks of this world ... tend to believe defeat is just a temporary setback."[1] Optimists see a bad situation as a challenge, so they try harder.

The most efficient way to move from pessimism to optimism is through what Seligman calls "explanatory style"—protecting yourself against failure or crisis by interpreting it in the most positive light. In our introductory example, the boss' comment elicited different explanations in the pessimist and optimist—both of whom, we're assuming, are valued employees. The pessimist begins allowing one unpleasant scenario after another—being fired, failing at a project, even being caught at marginally forbidden behavior—to career through his mind as an attempt to clarify the vague "meet me in my office" comment. His explanatory style is fueled by negative emotions like fear, failure, and guilt.

Meanwhile, the optimist is driving a different truck, one ruled by self-confidence and hopefulness. She expects the best and doesn't allow herself to attach negative fallout to a neutral statement. If anything's out of the ordinary, she tells herself, it's the *good* kind of unordinary—and she fully expects to benefit from it.

Let's take another scenario: an unsuccessful date. As opposed to wild conjecture (anticipating a firing or promotion based upon a single comment), this situation has a known outcome—failure. You meet someone new and you go out, but for a variety of reasons, the two of you just don't connect. Both of you look great and perform admirably, but in the end, you both go home knowing it won't work out.

---

1. Martin E.P. Seligman, *Learned Optimism* (New York: Knopf, 1991) p. 4. I'm indebted to Seligman and his valuable insights for the concept of explanatory style and most of the other good stuff in this chapter.

How you explain that failure to yourself says a lot about your personal outlook on life. The optimist will find positive reasons for the rejection. *He didn't seem comfortable with me*, she'll think. *He's not ready for a relationship right now. Or maybe he's more compatible with a different personality type.* She could even take it a step further: *Perhaps I intimidated him. I was simply too smart, too charming. He's just too stupid to know how great I am. Anyway, we didn't click, but that's because of him, not me.*

The pessimist, however, internalizes the rejection. *She didn't seem comfortable with me*, he'll think. Then he mentally dropkicks himself, blaming her discomfort on something he did wrong. Maybe he had bad breath. He must have been a dull conversationalist. His appearance was below-average. Whatever the reason, it was his fault.

In explaining the unsuccessful date to herself, the optimist refuses to accept a negative rationale. When one comes up mentally, she argues against it. Not so the pessimist. He fails to dispute his internal dialogue, allows a downbeat analysis of the date to run its course, and ends up attributing the bad experience to his own shortcomings. When the date ends, each of them runs into a wall— *he/she didn't seem comfortable with me*—but approaches it differently. The pessimist sees the wall, recognizes it (he's been here before), and just stops. Turns around and goes home. Race over. The optimist pauses momentarily at the wall, then starts climbing. Thinking of constructive reasons why the date didn't go well, she eventually reaches the top, drops to the other side, and starts moving again. She'll run a good race.

The trick is to anticipate the negative explanations and turn from them when they arrive. How? Gather evidence against your self-defeating thoughts. When "it's my fault" starts to emerge after the date, shut it out by remembering the people who *do* like you, who find you interesting, who enjoy being around you. Then, come up with different explanations for the failure (i.e. "She's *so* not ready for a relationship right now") and start arguing with the bad thoughts. Distract yourself from them.

Some people keep regurgitating the negative explanations like an anti-mantra—*something's wrong with me, something's wrong with me, something's wrong with me*—and before long, they believe it. When those thoughts arrive, set them aside. Find something else to occupy your mind. The goal is not only to take charge of what you think, but also to control when you think it.[2]

WHAT ABOUT WORRY?

Worry is closely related to pessimism. It's a natural response, closely aligned with our "fight or flight" instinct. When faced with a potentially dangerous situation, we have an emergency impulse to either: 1) defend ourselves or 2) scream like a girl and run away. Problem is, we aren't real good at the first option, ninjas and vampire slayers aside. We're slow. Our teeth are dull, our nails aren't particularly sharp, and we're not able to, for instance, confuse predators by expelling foul clouds of ink, like an octopus.

Which is a shame, really, because that would be cool.

So we try a different "fight or flight" tactic—control. Physically speaking, we turn to weaponry. We learned to forge steel and harness gunpowder in order to control dangerous animals and other humans. Mentally, we exert control another way. It's called worry.

In some situations, worry is good for us. People become more efficient and productive upon encountering situational anxiety. It's what drives us to roll up our sleeves and finish a project on a tight deadline. It allows us to keep a level head during a medical emergency. Situational anxiety is completely natural. It's fueled by adrenaline, lasts for a brief period of time, and occurs proportionately to the circumstance.

2. These insights also from Seligman, p. 89-90.

But there's also a bad kind of worry that's driven by insecurity rather than external forces. It's destructive instead of helpful and tends to blow things out of proportion. While situational anxiety wears off, destructive anxiety is persistent. It breaks you down physically, leaving sleepless nights, headaches, ulcers, depression, or even a suppressed immune system in its wake. Not good.

Again, it helps to put it in real-life terms. It's late at night, you're asleep in bed, and suddenly you're startled awake by the noise of breaking glass. Goodbye, grogginess. Your heart races, your palms sweat, and your breathing becomes shallow and slightly labored. That's good—the "fight or flight" response has kicked in. But should you find yourself experiencing the same physical sensations upon, for instance, discovering a coffee stain on your pants on your way to work (unfortunately, not your typical "fight or flight" situation), then the anxiety has gone too far.

For most of us, destructive worry creeps up when something occurs that makes us feel like we're losing control. Maybe we're burdened by an overwhelming project at work. As the responsibilities stack up and our sense of control diminishes, we feebly attempt to regain it by asking "what if?" *What if I can't get everything done on time? What if it makes the company lose money? What if I get fired? What if I can't pay my bills, and they repossess my house, and I find myself deranged and homeless on the streets of Manhattan, smoking used cigarette butts and begging for change?* Worry is our way of preparing ourselves to face the unknown by focusing on the worst possible outcome. It's like personal damage control because we feel honest relief when things don't turn out as bad as we thought.

The problem is that the end result—the relief—is not proportionate to the process. Being pleasantly surprised when you don't end up homeless after a stressful day at work doesn't exactly cancel out the ulcers you developed along the way.

HOW CAN I STOP WORRYING?

It's hard, because many people are chronic worriers. Telling them to cut back on anxiety is like telling someone to stop digesting food. Where would you even start?

There's a chance these extreme worriers suffer from Generalized Anxiety Disorder (GAD), which is said to strike more than four million Americans every year.[3] It's a chronic condition, characterized by six months or more of exaggerated stress at a level much more severe than what's considered normal. GAD sufferers worry about money, health, family, or work—even when those areas of life are trouble-free. They teeter on the edge of depression and may even entertain suicidal thoughts. If you fall into this category, the following suggestions probably won't help much. Talk to your physician about it. Describe how you feel and any symptoms that accompany your worry (aches and pains, insomnia, fatigue). The answer might be professional care, cognitive therapy, or medication—or some combination of the three.

IF YOUR WORRY IS LESS SEVERE, HERE ARE A FEW STEPS YOU CAN TAKE TO REGAIN CONTROL:

Check your medicine cabinet. Some prescription meds and over-the-counter products like nasal sprays, diet pills, and decongestants can generate feelings of anxiety.

Cut back on the caffeine. Because it stimulates your nervous system, too much caffeine may also increase nervousness. Go figure.

Exercise regularly. When stress levels rise and you feel like there's just not enough time in the day to get things done, one of the first victims is regular exercise. Bad move. Exercising regularly keeps you physically healthy, and it pumps up your mental well-being, too.

Learn how to relax. Activities like prayer, deep breathing, listening

3. Statistics from National Institute of Mental Health Web Site: "Facts About Generalized Anxiety Disorder" (posted April 9, 2004, at *www.nimh.nih.gov/publicat/gadfacts.cfm*).

to soothing music or doing yoga all are powerful stress-breakers. Find some way to take your mind off the worry and relax, even if it's something as simple as counting backward from one hundred.

Give worry a time and place. Some mental health experts actually recommend chronic worriers allow themselves a controlled, self-regulated anxiety session once a day—but on *their* terms. Designate a specific time and place to worry about stuff. When that time comes, spend a few minutes thinking about your worries and what you should do about them. Make a checklist or devise a plan of action. Focus on what you can do to take care of it. Then return to your day. If any other worries crop up, sweep them into the corner until your next "worry session."

The most important thing to remember when anxiety creeps up is to take action. When the piles on your desk grow to high-rise level, find a way to work more efficiently or delegate. Do medical research online if you're confronted by a family sickness. Take charge of your finances when money gets tight. Do something—anything—to help you exert some control over your anxiety. Just sitting around marinating in worry is the worst thing you can do.

FINAL WORDS

There are plenty of reasons to strive for an optimistic, worry-protected life. For one thing, you're more fun to be around—we'd all rather hang out with Tigger than Eeyore. Secondly, it's healthier. Research suggests optimists live longer. You'll have fewer physical or emotional problems, higher pain tolerance, increased energy, and a lower risk of premature death.[4] So lighten up.

4. "What's Your Outlook? The Benefits of Positive Thinking," *Mayo Clinic: Healthy Living Center: Healthy Aging Center* (posted September 18, 2002, at *www.mayoclinic.com/findinformation/healthylivingcenter/index.cfm*).

CHAPTER TEN

ESTABLISH YOUR OWN COOLNESS WITH AN AMAZING CARD TRICK

Thanks to the inevitable increase in baldness, paunch, and distance in years from hip teenagers, it's hard for a thirty-year-old to remain cool. This descent from relevance can't really be stopped, but it can be resisted, in minor increments, by projecting an aura of mystery. Tell people you have a tattoo but refuse to show them where it is. Say enigmatic things like "That reminds me of this sticky night in Amsterdam, but I don't want to talk about it." And learn to perform an amazing card trick.

Which trick? Glad you asked. It's a trick known in the magic world by several names, including Find the Card, the Twenty-One-Card Trick, the Eleventh Card, or Sim Sala Bim. It works due to a mathematical principle rather than a stacked deck or sleight-of-hand, so anyone can master it almost immediately and perform it in an impromptu setting. It'll take a little practice, some refined mid-trick patter, and more than a little attitude, but when you do it right, it always works. And it makes you cool.

THE SETUP

The goal is to have the spectator pick out a card from a group of twenty-one. You won't be told specifically which card it is, but you'll eventually find out. From there, you'll be able to reveal your knowledge via a number of mind-boggling scenarios. It's quite the puzzler.

Begin with twenty-one cards out of any deck. Doesn't matter which cards they are—any twenty-one will do. For credibility's sake, you might let your audience count out the initial twenty-one cards for you, in order to keep you from any pre-trick monkey business. Not that you'd need it.

Deal the cards, face-up, into three vertical columns of seven cards each. Distribute the cards horizontally: Card 1, Card 2, Card 3. Card 4 is laid in the same column as Card 1, overlapping it slightly. Card 5 overlaps Card 2, and so on. Continue until you've dealt out all twenty-one cards into three columns, seven cards deep. The dealing sequence is important to the trick, so don't accidentally deal two cards at once or distribute the cards top-to-bottom instead of across.

Ask someone to mentally select a card from one of the columns. Then have him indicate which column his card is resting in—left, middle, or right. You don't need to know suit, number, or anything else. Only the column.

Once the column has been indicated, square the three columns up (this is done much easier when the cards overlap) and stack them together. The spectator's column must be placed between the other two. For instance, if he indicates Column C, then assemble them in your hand with A on bottom, C in the middle, and B on top. Do this quickly and without fanfare, and your spectator won't notice you've reordered the columns.

Deal the cards out again, just like the first time. Again, have the person indicate which column his chosen card appears in. Then square them up and stack them together—the spectator's column goes between the other two.

Deal out the cards once again, same procedure, and have the person indicate his column. He will point to the middle column, and the card he chose at the beginning of the trick will be the card—card number 11—in the precise middle of the group of twenty-one. Take note of this card, then gather them up in order. **(NOTE:** *Occasionally, due to a quirk in card placement, the chosen card will not yet have "migrated" to the middle by this step. If your spectator indicates that his card is still in an outside column, simply repeat the step one more time. Then you'll be set.)*

So here's what you've got: A stack of twenty-one cards, and the card your spectator chose is the eleventh from the top (and, as it were, the eleventh from the bottom). You've arrived at this card via the wonders of a mathematical principle. It's a long, intricate explanation, using a combination of algebraic formulas that a) I'm too lazy to take the time to understand, and b) I'm not interested in going into anyway. I doubt you feel much differently. So just trust me on this—by making three piles three times and keeping the indicated pile in the middle of the pack, you automatically place the chosen card in the center of your twenty-one-card deck. There will be ten cards ahead of it and ten cards behind. Magic!

THE PAYOFF

What you do next depends on how tricky you want to be. A number of "reveals" are available to you, variations on ways to show the spectator his eleventh card. Like most things in life, the more creative the reveal, the better. Here are three options.

1) EASIEST. Pick a word or phrase that consists of either ten or eleven letters, then deal out one card per letter, stopping with the selected eleventh card. For instance, you can use the ten-letter phrase "Y-O-U-R C-A-R-D I-S," revealing the eleventh card after you've finished spelling. Or, choose an eleven-letter word like "Abracadabra" and spell it out: "A-B-R-A-C-A-D-A-B-R-A," wherein the card is exposed on the final "A." While any eleven-letter name, word, or phrase works, it's best to stick with something that makes sense—"big fat biker," for instance, may earn points for originality, but it'll probably just confuse your spectator.[1]

2) NEXT EASIEST. First, tell your audience that you're going to turn over the cards one by one in order to find the chosen card. Then start peeling them off the deck and placing them face-up on the table. You know the correct card is the eleventh one, but keep peeling until you get to Card 13 (mentally take note of Card 11 as it's dealt). Then say, "The next card I turn over will be your card." The spectator will be feeling all patronizing and superior because his card is staring him in the face from the discard pile.

But you, the wily conjurer, will take advantage of his confidence by offering to make a friendly wager on the outcome. He'll agree. You'll shake hands, and then, instead of turning over the incorrect fourteenth card that's next on the deck—as he'll most likely assume—you'll reach down and turn over Card 11, the one that's already on the table. Flip it over and smile.[2]

---

1. Unless, of course, your spectator really *is* a big fat biker, in which case your trick will likely insult rather than confuse. In which case you should wrap things up with a hasty disappearing act.

2. Unless, of course, you're dealing with another big fat biker. In this scenario, flip it over and run.

3) *MOST DIFFICULT BUT QUITE ASTONISHING IF YOU CAN PULL IT OFF.* The "reveal" in this case is made to look like it's under the spectator's control. Fortunately, that's only the way it'll *appear*, since you will, in fact, be working the table like an evil puppetmaster, manipulating the cards at will. You've got to play this one like butter, and you can only do it once. Any more than that, and your audience may catch on to your trickery. Here's how it works:

Start by placing the cards face-down on the table in groups of two, one on top of the other in the shape of an X. With twenty-one cards, you'll be able to make ten piles; one card will be left over. Pay attention to the location of the eleventh card—for our purposes here, we'll call that the Star Pile. *You must remember which pile is the Star Pile, and which of its two cards is the eleventh card.*

Show the one remaining card to your spectator. "This isn't your card, is it?" you'll ask. He'll say no. "Good," you'll reply. "Just checking." (Clever little script I've written here, is it not?) Toss the unwanted card aside with panache.

Have your spectator choose five out of the ten piles by pointing to them. If one of the piles he points to is the Star Pile, then quickly gather up and remove the other five. If he does *not* include the Star Pile among his picks, then remove each of the piles he chooses. It's important not to say anything beforehand like "Tell me which piles to take away." Don't limit yourself to a certain action—whether you keep piles or remove them depends on whether or not the Star Pile is indicated.

You have five piles left, one of which is the Star Pile. Repeat the previous step, only ask your participant to choose three piles this time. Same process—either remove or retain depending on which piles he singles out.

You have two piles left. "Choose one pile," you'll say. If he points to the Star Pile, it stays; remove the remaining one. If he indicates the other pile, remove it. The two cards of the Star Pile will be the only ones left.

Have him chose one of the two cards remaining. This is where you need to remember which card—top or bottom—is the eleventh card. If he points to it, simply pick it up and show it to him: "Exactly!" you'll say. "This is indeed your card." If he points to the other card, then remove it from the table. The remaining card will be the one the spectator chose at the very beginning of the trick. Nice job, Houdini.

Act nonchalant as the audience hoots in applause. After all, this kind of thing happens all the time to great magicians.

By slyly making the spectator think he's controlling the exclusion of certain piles of cards, you're setting up a major payoff when the last card on the table—the one he seems to have picked at random—is the actual card he chose but never revealed to you way back at the beginning of the process. Again, you'll only be able to do this once. Otherwise you run the risk of the audience catching on to the fact that sometimes you're eliminating the indicated piles and sometimes you're keeping them. Perform the trick with swift, smooth confidence, then move on to the next unsuspecting victim.

FINAL WORDS

This is a great first-time card trick because it's so easy. There's no sleight-of-hand involved, no palming, no deck-stacking, no special cards. You can perform it spur-of-the-moment—resting in the confidence that there's no chance the trick won't work when you deal and gather the cards correctly.[3]

Like most card tricks, presentation is key. Even though the trick is

---

3. In fact, you don't even have to have twenty-one cards. Any odd number will work, so long as you divide them into an odd number of rows and an odd number of columns (for instance: nine total cards separated into three columns of three cards apiece). After three dealings, the chosen card will always end up in the exact middle of your set.

as simple as knowing how to count, treat it as if you're completely at ease with the mind-blowing mystery. Don't tell anyone in advance what's going to happen. And don't explain how you did it once the trick's over. Do it once, flash a mischievous grin, and walk away, shrouded in secrecy.

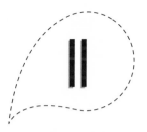

CHAPTER ELEVEN

BLING-FREE IS THE WAY TO BE: LIVE BENEATH YOUR MEANS

It's estimated that 80 percent of America's self-made millionaires—by which we mean those who have pulled themselves up by their bootstraps, rather than being born into money or having it given to them because they can throw a ninety-seven-mile-an-hour fastball left-handed—have achieved economic independence by being frugal. They're rich because they don't spend much money. They buy only what they need and only what they can afford.

The temptation is to do the opposite—to live *above* our means. We buy too much stuff. Not because we need it. Sometimes, not because we even want it. We buy because we *can*. And the funny thing is that even though we make personal decisions based on this mindset, it's not really a factor in our social decisions. Consider the people closest to you—your friends, your fellow employees, your family. What forms the foundation for those relationships? What's the joint that keeps you together? None of us would chalk the connection up to material things: "I'm friends with Jessica because she has an awesome car." Or "I like to spend time with my sister on account of her fantastic furniture."

Possessions don't matter nearly as much as we think they do, which brings us to a financial virtue too many adults fail to practice: the art of living beneath your means.

THE PROBLEM

Here's how it happens. Joe graduates from college, bumps around a few years, then eventually finds a nice job with a company looking for energetic young talent. He starts pulling down a decent salary. Within a few weeks, Joe's got more money than he's ever had in his life. So he does the obvious—he goes out and buys himself a brand-new car. He didn't exactly need one, as his 1998 Civic got him to and from work just fine and with good fuel economy. No, Joe made the purchase simply because he suddenly had the cash for it. Because a hotshot young businessman really shouldn't be driving around in a dated Honda, should he?

So, is Joe wrong? Not necessarily. Is what he did morally repugnant? To some, maybe, but not to most. Is it smart? Well, no. Generally speaking, it's not smart.

Why? Because, like most people, Joe won't stop with just the car. Soon he'll fall in love with someone. She'll have an equally nice job and nice car. The two of them will pool their money, grin at how much they're both raking in, and began to live the DINK lifestyle— Double-Income, No Kids. They'll buy the biggest and newest house they can afford. They'll decorate it just like pages 32–36 of the latest Pottery Barn catalog. They'll grow accustomed to eating out and start paying too much for entertainment.

Then they'll decide to have kids. And when Junior finally arrives, they're in a pretty serious financial pickle.

More and more young mothers these days are opting to become full-time, stay-at-home moms, at least for the first few years of their kids' lives. Many moms want to—really, *really* want to—but can't because they're living above their double-income means. For these young families, cutting back to a single income is absolutely impossible without a drastic lifestyle change. And lifestyle change is hard. So they end up shelling out thousands a year to keep the kid in daycare because they can't afford to do anything else. Their lifestyle of consumerism has impacted their family, and that's a pretty good signal that things need to change.

THE SOLUTION

Changing our spending habits, however, is hard. It's much easier said than done, because our spending habits are a part of us—they begin to develop as soon as we receive and cash our first paycheck. Many of us have been on the road to financial trouble for a long time, but there's no need to keep driving when we know the destination won't be any fun. It's time to consider getting off at the next exit, and the best strategy for this is to adopt a frame of mind that's not always popular in today's culture.

INSIST ON SPENDING LESS THAN YOU MAKE. HERE'S HOW:

Budget your spending. Decide what kind of standard of living you want to adopt and figure out how much money it'll take to do so. Make sure that amount is less than what you earn. Stick to it, and save or invest whatever remains. If you bring home $3,000 a month, budget for $2,500. The rest goes in the bank. (For more about budgeting, see chapter 19.)

Look ahead. Consider your future before making a big financial decision, particularly when buying cars or houses. A thirty-year mortgage is a looooong time. You may be able to afford it now on a combined income, but do you always want to be dependent on both incomes? If you're married and planning to have kids, this is extremely important to consider. Think before spending.

Stop buying so much crap. This one's easy. Do you really need two soft drinks every day? That tall latte? *Another* pair of Skechers? You'd be amazed how little we can live on comfortably. You don't have to set up your own monastery or anything, but everyone can find a few areas—non-necessities like entertainment, dining out, or name-brand clothing—that can be cut back.

Hide the gravy. Say you're making an entry-level $30,000 a year and living quite comfortably on that. Then you get a $5,000 raise. Woo! Do you go out immediately and lease a bigger, better apartment? Do you buy a newer car? Do you blow it on a vacation? Nope. If you're a good little boy or girl, you "hide" the money. Set up an automatic withdrawal with your bank, then direct deposit the extra into a retirement plan or mutual fund. You haven't needed it thus far, so why spend it just because it's there? It's gravy. Hide that $5K, and you'll never miss it. Do this for a few years, and you'll be in better financial shape than you could have ever imagined.

FINAL WORDS

There's nothing wrong, of course, with making money. It's a necessity, so go ahead—set whatever financial goals you want to, then work hard to reach them. Earn as much as you can, but remember: If you're accustomed to spending more than you make, then it doesn't matter what numbers are on your paycheck—you'll always fall short of your goals.

The secret to living beneath your means is to question everything you spend money on, from discretionary stuff like gym memberships to basics like food and shelter. Ask yourself: Do I really need this, or do I just want it? Answer honestly. Make a habit of it, and you'll be on your way to capping consumerism.

And when you get there? Be proud. You're different from most of us.

12

PREPARE FOR THE WORST WITH A PROPERLY STOCKED MEDICINE CABINET

In 1998, more than 130,000 people in Great Britain were hospitalized after tripping over their carpet. Another 30,000 hurt themselves by falling off a ladder. And seventy deaths and 100,000 hospital visits resulted from misuse of tools. Clearly, British homes are dangerous places.[1]

So ... are the Brits just clumsy? Possibly, but not any more so than Americans. If anything, they're just better at keeping track of these kinds of statistics. You know how they say that 90 percent of all accidents happen within five miles of your home? What they forget to mention is that most actually occur *inside* the home, and

1. "Warning: Your Pants Can Kill," *Guardian Unlimited* (posted May 30, 2000, at *www.guardian. co.uk/health/story/0,3605,319998,00.html*).

evidently involve ladders and carpet.

Which brings us to this conclusion: Every responsible adult who lives somewhere—homeowners, apartment dwellers, moochers subsisting on their parents' dime—needs to be fully prepared to deal with injuries and illnesses that take place in the home. That means you need a carefully stocked medicine cabinet. Let's get to the details.

STUFF YOU NEED

Minor injury supplies. Let's say you fall off a ladder and cut your knee (clumsy Brit!). You don't want to then limp all over the house, trailing blood around while searching for a Band-Aid. Your medicine cabinet should have all the basics of minor wound management in one place, including adhesive bandages, gauze and sterile tape, hydrogen peroxide (the fun stuff that bubbles as it cleans the germs out of your wound), and an ice pack. *FUN TIP:* A bag of frozen peas also makes an effective ice pack, just in case. But it looks weird.

Pain reliever/Fever reducer. Most professionals recommend keeping two types of pain relief products on hand. One should be an ibuprofen-based or aspirin product that acts as an anti-inflammatory—these are ideal for toothaches, muscle pulls, menstrual cramps, arthritis, etc. The other should be a nonaspirin pain reliever like Tylenol, which is most effective for general aches and pains, fever reduction, and headaches.

Antibiotic ointment. A triple antibiotic cream, such as Neosporin, is the best infection protection available for minor cuts and scrapes. For faster, germ-free healing, simply apply a thin coat beneath a bandage.

Pepto-Bismol or its equivalent. No one likes to talk about it, but at some point we all get a little quake in the belly. Which means a product to treat diarrhea, nausea, indigestion, and heartburn is essential.

Syrup of Ipecac. Pray you never have to use this, but keep it on hand just in case. Ipecac is used to induce vomiting in case of accidental poisoning or ingestion of an unknown product. **IMPORTANT TIP:** Use it only after calling poison control and being instructed to do so. Some chemicals like bleach or other corrosives do greater harm on the way back up than they do going down.

Decongestants and antihistamines. These are the products that relieve cold and allergy symptoms. Some professionals only recommend buying cold and cough medicines when they're needed, since there are so many varieties. That's your call. If you suffer often from allergies or deal with a perpetual stuffy nose, then it makes sense to keep an over-the-counter antihistamine on hand.

Cough medicines. There are two kinds: suppressants and expectorants. Cough suppressants help quiet the kind of dry, irritating cough that keeps you up at night and annoys your friends. Expectorants help loosen chest congestion (also known, delicately, as "inducing phlegm"). Though a little unpleasant, this kind of coughing helps clear all that extra infection-prone phlegm from your lungs, so it's a good thing to do. Many cough medicines combine a suppressant and expectorant into a single dose. These types of over-the-counter meds are intended for minor coughs only, so if you have one that persists for more than a few days, see a doctor.

Hydrocortisone cream. The strongest anti-itching cream available, so keep this around to treat skin rashes or itchiness due to minor irritations and inflammations, eczema, insect bites, poison ivy, etc.

Tweezers. For splinters, in case you were wondering. A

magnifying glass also helps. And while we're on the subject, here's a secret: One of the least painful and most effective means of splinter removal is to apply clear tape to the area, then carefully peel it off—splinter included.

Thermometer. These days, you really can't beat a good digital thermometer. They're much faster, more accurate, and easier to use and read than the kind your mom had. A good thermometer is worth the investment, especially if you have kids.

Sunscreen. Pasty and white is better than wrinkled and cancerous any day. Minimum SPF should be fifteen.

First-Aid manual. Unless, of course, you've memorized one.

STUFF YOU DON'T NEED

Expired medications. Some products lose their potency as they age (case in point: Aerosmith), but a few liquid meds may begin to evaporate and become *more* powerful. It doesn't happen automatically at the expiration date, but it's safest not to take a chance.

Old prescriptions. Anything you've had more than two years is suspect. It's tempting to save half-used prescriptions for ailments you no longer have but conceivably could suffer from again in the future. But self-medication can sometimes do more harm than good. And while you're at it, toss any unlabeled medicine or medicine prescribed for someone else.

Damaged goods. Remove the following items from your medicine cabinet: Hydrogen peroxide that no longer bubbles. Aspirin that crumbles or smells vinegary. Any medicine that has been the victim of water leaks. Any medicine that has begun to degrade, discolor, separate, or form a gooey residue. In fact, if *anything* in your home has begun forming a gooey residue, it's probably a good idea to get rid of it.

Expired condoms. Most are good for four to five years past the date of manufacture and don't just fall to pieces the day they expire. But the name of the game is safety, right? Err on the side of caution. Incidentally, condoms with spermicides are good for only eighteen months to two years (which is when the spermicide expires, not the condom).

STUFF YOU PROBABLY HAVEN'T THOUGHT ABOUT BUT SHOULD

Green tea. The ancient Chinese and Japanese used to regard green tea as a medicine, and we're just now beginning to understand why, as scientists keep discovering all these health benefits associated with it. Green tea contains a powerful antioxidant compound called polyphenol. Scientists think polyphenols help prevent cancer from forming and may shrink cancer cells that are already present. Green tea may also protect against heart disease, boost the immune system, prevent the formulation of blood clots and strokes, and even guard against digestive and respiratory infections. There's also evidence it may help avoid cavities, reduce cholesterol, and give you X-ray vision. (Okay, went too far on that last one.) But green tea is practically a super-powered beverage. Health-conscious adults would do well to add a steaming mug to the daily routine.[2]

Vitamin C supplements. Recent research has discovered a link between vitamin C deficiency and a bunch of health problems, including cataracts, stomach and esophageal cancer, and rheumatoid arthritis. A lack of vitamin C can also lead to minor annoyances like nosebleeds, easy bruising, and bleeding gums. And large doses of it (500 to 1,000 mg a day) may lessen symptoms and decrease duration of the common cold. You can get your minimum daily allowance of vitamin C by drinking orange juice and eating fresh strawberries,

---

2. Some forms of nonherbal black teas also contain polyphenols, but in smaller amounts.

oranges, and grapefruit, or you can take one of the countless vitamin C supplements on the market.

Soap and sanitizing gels. Speaking of colds, we're all walking around with bacteria on our hands, and when we touch doorknobs and water faucets and soft drink machines, we're depositing our own personal germs and collecting those of our neighbors. So, yuck. Regular hand-washing is the best way to fight this, keeping germs and the diseases they cause from spreading. The Centers for Disease Control and Prevention recommends vigorously scrubbing your hands in warm water for at least fifteen seconds to effectively remove germs. If soap's not readily available, an antibacterial hand sanitizer gel will do the trick, all while making your hands smell like vanilla mango. Or something equally manly.[3]

FINAL WORDS

To keep your medicine cabinet from becoming a burial ground for old prescription bottles, goo-developing creams, and yellowed bandages, give it a good reorganization every year or so.

And contrary to popular belief, the bathroom really isn't the best place to house your medicine cabinet. Most medical products store best in cool, dry environments, not warm and humid ones. Consider collecting everything in a big plastic container and storing it on the top shelf of an interior closet, out of the reach of children.

Your home medicine cabinet should be well-organized, easy-to-access, and regularly updated. Because we all know carpet can be tricky.

---

3. A warning, though: Our love of antibacterial products may be in danger of being taken too far. For one thing, many diseases are viral in nature, and antibacterial soap doesn't have any effect on them. Secondly, some bacteria are good for us, but we're killing them off with all our mango-smelling soap. Thirdly, scientists worry that our use of bacteria-killing agents may lead to the development of bacterial "superbugs" over the long term—really, really bad germs that are resistant to our soaps and gels. Furthermore, in October 2002, researchers released the results of a study finding that soaps with antibacterial compounds don't work any better than regular soap products in killing germs. Source: Jim Ritter, "Anti-Germ Soap No Better Than Plain Kind," *Chicago Sun-Times* (posted October 24, 2002, at *www.suntimes.com/output/health/cst-nws-soap24.html*).

CHAPTER THIRTEEN

BLEND YOUR WAY TO HAPPINESS WITH A BUTT-KICKIN' FRUIT SMOOTHIE

Fruit smoothies are the mixed drink of the new millennium.
Despite their most obvious benefit—which is the deliciously
calming way the word "smoothie" slides off your puckered lips
(seriously … say "smoothie" five times real fast and darn it if you
don't feel better about life in general)—these are quick, tasty treats
to replenish your fast-food-slogged body. Smoothies are much more
than a fun drink; they're good for you, too.

Only one out of four Americans eats the recommended serving

of five fruits and vegetables on a daily basis.[1] Yet eating a regular diet rich in fruits and vegetables can boost energy, fortify the immune system, and possibly even decrease the risk of cancer by nearly one-third.[2] "An apple a day" is right.

Best way to get those servings? A smoothie. When made properly (that is, when made without multiple scoops of Ben & Jerry's Cherry Garcia, which, unfortunately, does not qualify as fruit), smoothies are low in calories, low in fat, and high in vitamins, minerals, antioxidants, fiber, and overall hipness.

MAIN INGREDIENTS

A well-made smoothie has anywhere from two to four basic ingredients, depending on your taste. For the purist, there are two—and only two—building blocks to a good smoothie: fruit (one of which should be a banana) and juice. Drinkers with less refined palates often choose to add a thickening agent like yogurt, sorbet, or milk to the mix. And those who depend on the smoothie for a refreshing after-workout nectar like to blend in crushed ice cubes for texture.

With the right ingredients, however, you can achieve a smooth, refreshing texture without the milk, ice, yogurt, or any nonfruit ingredients that add extra calories and carbs to your drink. What are those ingredients? Simple: A banana (any degree of ripeness will do), frozen fruit (buy it in a bag at any grocery store), and juice (choose your poison, but make sure it's 100 percent juice, and not, for instance, Grape Fanta).

And you need a good blender.

Bananas. Because they provide a sweet, natural counter to the tartness of most fruits, bananas are key to a good smoothie. For general eating purposes, most people lose interest once bananas get

---

1. From the National Cancer Institute's "Eat 5 to 9 a Day for Better Health" Web Site, located at *www.5aday.gov*.
2. Centers for Disease Control and Prevention (CDC) 1998 Behavioral Risk Factor Surveillance Data.

overly ripe and start spotting brown. Not so for smoothies. Put your browning bananas in the fridge. This stops the ripening process (at the cooler temperature, they'll still turn brown on the outside—really dark, nasty brown—but maintain firmness and taste), and these refrigerated bananas can become smoothie fodder within a day or two. It doesn't hurt that they're already cold when their time comes. (Just don't let anyone see you drop that discolored banana into the blender. And don't forget to peel it first.)

Fruit. If you're mixing in a banana, almost any other fruit will form a flavorsome complement. Use your imagination, and use frozen fruit. Most general-interest fruit is available in your grocer's freezer—peaches, strawberries, blueberries, raspberries. Smoothie aficionados pay particular attention to bags of mixed fruit. Try a berry blend, which contains a combination of the three berries listed above and is an excellent source of fiber. Another favorite is a melon blend, which typically packages honeydew, cantaloupe, peaches, and blueberries together. Feel free to pop any fresh fruit you have into the freezer for an hour or two before use. Using already frozen fruit keeps you from having to feed ice into the mixture (which can be difficult on the blender and waters down your drink). The fruit cools down the smoothie and gives you a softer, consistently slushy texture.

NOTE: Don't let the frozen fruit rule keep you from also adding whatever fresh fruit you have on hand. Kiwis make great smoothie ingredients, as do fresh nectarines, pineapples, mangoes, and pretty much anything else.

Juice. Most smoothie recipes call for orange juice, but again, feel free to experiment. These days, there are tons of mixed juices (strawberry-grape, orange-pineapple-banana, cranberry-mixed berry) which make great smoothie bases. If you're using frozen fruit, then cold, liquid juice is fine—simply add it to the blender along with the fruit. If the fruit is fresh, not frozen, it's a good idea to use frozen juice concentrate—the kind that comes in the little cylindrical containers. Just add a little water to dilute the concentrate and enjoy the nice, slushy goodness.

ALTERNATE INGREDIENTS

Some people like to give their smoothies a little extra zip in addition to fruit and juice. While these alternate ingredients aren't necessary for proper texture or taste—the right combination of frozen fruit and bananas should handle that—they can turn a regular smoothie into a smoothie with kick. They'll also add calories, so keep that in mind. Here are a few of the favorites:

Yogurt. For a thick, smooth consistency, consider adding a half-cup of nonfat yogurt. Plain or vanilla provides a nice balance to the fruit, but you can also get great results from flavored versions. Yogurt is an excellent source of protein, riboflavin, and vitamin B-12 and is considered a better source of calcium than a glass of milk. It helps strengthen the immune system by adding healthy bacterial cultures to your stomach. (Try not to use the phrase "bacterial cultures" while serving your smoothie, though. Some things are better left unsaid.)

Milk. The old standby for making stuff creamier. Adding milk is a good way to load a smoothie up with protein and calcium. Using reduced fat (2 percent) or skim milk is the best bet for keeping the fat grams and calories at a reasonable level.

Sorbet. A frozen dessert with high fruit content, sorbet makes an excellent smoothie ingredient. Plus, it's dairy-free, so a sorbet smoothie will be safe for the lactose-intolerant or those who can't handle milk or dairy products. Sorbet comes in a variety of fruit flavors and is the secret ingredient to some of the most savory smoothies. Sherbet is pretty much the same thing as sorbet, taste-wise, but it contains milk.

FINAL WORDS: RECIPES

Following are a handful of easy recipes for smoothie-making. Reward yourself. Impress your friends. Unpack that blender you've never used. And remember that smoothie recipes are just suggestions. Like rules, they're made to be broken.[3]

BANANA-BERRY

20 oz. orange juice

1 banana, peeled

1 cup frozen strawberries

Blend and serve. Makes two large servings.

BREAKFAST BLEND

1 banana, peeled

12 oz. pineapple juice

1/2 cup lowfat vanilla yogurt

1 cup frozen strawberries

Blend and serve. Makes two small servings.

BERRY PEACHY

20 oz. orange juice

1 banana

1/2 cup fresh peaches

1 cup frozen mixed berries (strawberries, raspberries, blueberries)

Blend and serve. Makes two large servings.

3. Except for the important rules, like not harming your fellow man or taking his property. And stuff like stop signs. And the one about waiting an hour before swimming after you eat. Don't break those rules.

GREEN GIANT

3 kiwi fruit, peeled and sliced

Half a banana

1 cup skim milk

1 tbsp. fresh lemon juice

1 large scoop lime sorbet

Blend the kiwi, banana, milk, and juice about ten seconds, then add the sorbet and mix on low until smooth. Makes two servings.

CANTABERRY TALE

20 oz. cranberry-grape juice

1 banana

1 cup frozen strawberries

1 cup fresh cantaloupe, diced

Blend and serve. Makes two large servings.

CHAPTER FOURTEEN

YOUR 401(K) SHOULD BE AGGRESSIVE BUT DIVERSIFIED

Let's say you graduate from college, kick around between Prague and the Koh Sahn Road for a couple of years, then come back to the States at twenty-four. You score a sweet job paying more than $35,000 a year. And because you're single and have few financial responsibilities (good job with that, by the way), you decide to put back a lot into your 401(k). Combining your monthly contributions with your generous employer match, you end up investing a total of $250 a month into your retirement plan. That's $3,000 a year. Boca Raton, here you come!

If you continue this trend for forty years, until the age of sixty-five, guess how much money you'll have? Assuming such variables as regular monthly contributions, no withdrawals or loans, 8 percent interest compounded monthly (which, even in a volatile market, is still a pretty reasonable long-term figure), and tax-deferred earnings, you can plan on a final account balance of nearly $900,000. Total amount you'll actually have invested? No more than $120,000, a lot of which came from your employer. Behold the power of the 401(k) and its trusty sidekick, compounded interest.[1]

401(K) BASICS

The example above is why 401(k) plans are still the best choice for the youngish investor. As far as investments go, they don't get any easier. Here's a quick primer on the theoretical virtues of the 401(k). If you already know how it works, feel free to skip ahead. Investment virgins? Read on.

In most cases, the company you work for can set aside a portion of your paycheck (this is called an "elective contribution") into a separate fund to help you save for retirement. Many employers will match part of your elective contribution up to a certain amount—for instance, a common corporate match is 50 percent of your contribution up to 6 percent of your salary. You pay no federal income tax on any contributions to your 401(k) or any income earned by those contributions (an *excellent* benefit, by the way) until you collect on the plan, which you aren't allowed to do until you're at least fifty-nine-and-a-half-years-old. This is pretty much the only time in life when your half-birthday means anything.

The money you set aside is combined with your company's match and used to purchase a variety of stocks, bonds, and money market investments. You'll usually have a bunch of options, each varying according to risk level and growth potential. You choose an

---

1. For those of you who slept through twelfth grade economics, *compounded interest* refers to the process of gaining interest on interest. In other words, the interest you earn on your investments is re-invested, which then allows you to earn new interest on top of old interest. Thus, your investment keeps building and building upon itself, and before you know it, you've got a potload of money.

investment approach, elect a certain amount to be taken from your paycheck, and watch your nest egg grow.

It's that easy, especially if you start while you're young.

That's why 401(k) plans are almost always a good idea for the young investor. But since most plans give you different options for distributing your money, the hard part is knowing what kind of strategy to pursue. ***HERE'S A TIP:*** Experts almost always advise young investors to be both aggressive and diversified in building their retirement portfolios. What does that mean? Read on.

BE AGGRESSIVE

You're young, which means now is the perfect time to plan for the future. Doesn't mean you need to start test-driving Winnebagos or eating at Golden Corral, but you do need to come up with a retirement strategy and stick to it. Don't wait. The sooner you start, the more time your money has to grow.

One way to be aggressive is to enroll for your 401(k) as soon as you're qualified (many companies require employees to work a certain number of months before eligibility kicks in). Using the example from the introduction, the difference between starting at age twenty-five and starting at age thirty is just $15,000 in total investments, but $300,000 in accumulated interest. Those last five years of compounding are *big*. Shaquille O'Neal big. Get in the game as quickly as you can.

The second step in aggressive investing is to contribute each month until you bleed. Maximize your plan—defer as much to your 401(k) as your employer will match. A common mistake employees make is failing to take advantage of their company match, not realizing that, in effect, the bigwigs are pretty much shoving free money into your account. We've already stated that some employers match 50 percent of contributions up to 6 percent of your salary. If that's the case, don't just set aside a paltry 2 or 3 percent. Scratch as much out of your employer as you can. Fork over 6 percent to get the full match. Then, just because your employer stops there doesn't mean you have to—you can give more, up to 15 percent of your income or $14,000.[2] The extra money each year won't be matched, but it does add up—a little bit year to year, a truckload decade to decade.

Step three in being aggressive involves your investment choices. Most 401(k) plans let you decide where to invest your money. You'll have several options. An easy way to evaluate investment options is by a simple risk/reward ratio. Aggressive, high-risk investments give you the opportunity for higher potential reward. Conservative, low-risk investments have less potential for growth, but let you sleep better at night.

Microsoft Chairman Bill Gates, who apparently has a few dollars to his name, once said he only looks at the price of Microsoft stock once a month—his focus is on the end game, not what's immediately in front of him. Same goes for investors in their twenties and early thirties. At this stage, your 401(k) is still in development mode; you're trying to build it up. For that reason, you should be willing to accept greater risk in exchange for a higher growth potential because you won't be needing the money for at least thirty years. So even if a certain stock or fund tanks for a year, you're still okay. Chances are, things will even out over the long haul.[3]

The rule for investors under forty is to be brave. Invest aggressively. This kind of strategy involves what is usually called a

2. This is the cap for 2005, an amount set by the IRS and adjusted annually to reflect cost-of-living increases. Your employer should keep you informed each time the amount changes.
3. But that's not *always* true. After all, you could have worked at Enron or Lucent or WorldCom or Tyco or some other high-tech bust from a few years back—and lost it all. Some companies offer a variety of funds to choose from and make their company match in straight-up cash. Unfortunately, others match with company stock, often refusing to let employees sell until they reach a certain age (such as fifty-five). That's no worry when the stock is doubling or tripling in value, but it's a big problem when the stock falls to pieces and your nest egg gets scrambled.

"growth portfolio." Such a plan is diversified among different types of stocks (which tend to fluctuate), with very few, if any, investments in more stable bonds and cash instruments. Growth funds maximize your investment over the long-term but can sometimes look ugly in the short-term—especially during a struggling economy. But history shows that, over the decades, the stock market will rise slowly but surely, despite the inevitable hiccups.

Put your money in, check it a month at a time rather than daily, and make sure you're nicely diversified. Which brings us, in a dazzling segue, to the next point ...

DIVERSIFY

Roger Boyce, an Enron employee living in Minneapolis, believed in the energy giant so much he put all of his 401(k) contributions into Enron stock. He got bonuses of Enron stock. His company match came in the form of stock. He lived and breathed and sweated Enron stock. And for several years, this living and breathing and sweating made him rich. He retired a millionaire. Then, when Enron collapsed, his $2 million portfolio dropped like an egg to a tile floor. The result was messy. Within days, it was worth less than $10,000.[4]

The Enron lesson: Eggs are fragile, and sometimes they break. Don't keep them all in one basket.

That's why you need to diversify your portfolio. Invest across different sectors of the marketplace, picking a variety of stocks instead of one single stock. Don't overinvest in a certain class of mutual fund (small caps, for instance) or a certain fund sector (technology, energy). Spread your investments out.

A good way to diversify is to include among your investments an index fund and an international growth fund. An index fund tries to match the return of a specified market index, usually the S & P

4. Catherine Valenti, "Retirement at Risk? 401(k) Losses in Wake of Enron's Collapse Could Inspire Changes," *ABCNews.com* (posted December 4, 2001).

500. In the last few years, index funds have regularly outperformed actively managed funds, which try to *beat* the market but don't always succeed (often charging higher fees in the process). Most 401(k) plans will offer at least one index fund among investment options.

An international fund manages a diversified portfolio of stock from companies located outside the United States (thereby ensuring at least part of your investment is not tied to the performance of the U.S. economy). A good plan is to designate money toward one of each of the above, if they're available, and then choose a couple more options, such as large-, mid-, or small-cap funds.

The goal is to broaden your investments. Diversify geography, diversify industry sectors, diversify fund managers, diversify everything. Gather as many eggs as you can, but spread them over several baskets. That way, you'll survive major economic swings, industry downfalls, and bankrupt companies. Even if one basket drops, you still have plenty to cook with.

FINAL WORDS

Start early. Take advantage of your company match and contribute until your wallet hurts. And invest smart, spreading the risk around. Keep these things in mind while you're young, and you'll be ready to retire in only, um, thirty-five to forty years. Give or take.

Woohoo.

CHAPTER FIFTEEN

HOW NOT TO FALL PREY TO ORGAN HARVESTERS OR URBAN LEGENDS

I was on a business trip to Las Vegas once and driving at night. A car approached me from some distance away. I was lucky to have seen it in the first place, because the vehicle didn't have its headlights on. Thoughtful driver that I am, I gave it the quick "hey, genius, turn your lights on" headlight flash as the car passed by. No sooner had I done that, then the darkened vehicle executed a sudden U-turn and latched on to my tail like skeeze on Paris Hilton. Perhaps they wanted to thank me for my good deed, but I have a feeling they intended to kill me as some sort of gang initiation. Just my luck.

As the villains approached me from behind, attempting to pass, they suddenly switched on their brights and jerked back behind me, swerving wildly. I gulped. Then they did it again: Lights. Tailgating.

Honking. Beginning to suspect some sort of danger, I checked the rearview mirror and caught the glint of a butcher knife behind my head. Yikes! There was a deranged killer rising up from my backseat to stab me! Those thoughtful tailgating gangbangers and their high beams had been keeping me safe.

I stopped at a deserted gas station to let the killer out, and the rest of the drive passed without incident. I made it to the hotel, unloaded my bags, and headed for the bar. As luck would have it, I encountered a shapely young blonde there. We struck up a conversation and immediately hit it off. We shared a few drinks. But I must have blacked out at some point, because suddenly I awoke in the bathtub of my hotel room, naked and surrounded by ice. So naturally I checked my email. "Don't move," an urgent message read. "Call 9-1-1 immediately. P.S.—We've got your kidneys. Bill Gates has promised us $1,000 for each one we deliver to him, plus a trip to Disney World. Forward this to everyone you know. This is not a hoax."

Blasted organ harvesters.

STITCHES, CATAPULTS, AND CORNBALLS

In our generation, during which IM has replaced the teenage slumber party and message boards the campfire, urban legends have become the stitches of our social fabric. They show up everywhere, from movies and television shows to our email inboxes. When told correctly, with supplemental flair and dramatic pause, they can—best-case scenario—win you a captive audience. More likely, though, they can catapult you straight to dorkhood with the forward of a chain email. "This may be too good to be true," you write ahead of a description of Bill Gates' charitable email tracking request, "but what if it's not?!?!?"

The answer, of course, is this: If it seems too good to be true, then you should have recognized it prior to outing yourself as a gullible cornball. So, fellow folklorists, here's something every grownup should know: how to recognize the urban legend.

Also: how not to be an inbox-clogging goof.

WHAT IT IS

An urban legend is simply a fictional story passed from one person to another and told as if true (i.e. this really happened—a friend of a friend swears on it!). The federal tax on email? Urban legend. Mall parking lot rapists who knock out their victims with ether-laced perfume? Urban legend. The Neiman Marcus cookie recipe, HIV-infected needles in pay phones, the anti-religious misdeeds of Madalyn Murray O'Hair? Urban legends all.[1]

While a legend itself may be grounded in truth, it's too good or too horrible or too funny to be real. But whether it's true or not doesn't really matter. What matters is that a story is *alleged* to be true without any real evidence. And the "this really happened to a friend" disclaimer? Sorry. Doesn't count.

Urban legends are a kind of folklore, the traditional beliefs, superstitions, and tales of the common people. These legends tend to evolve into different animals during the telling; as a story is passed from one individual to another, each storyteller may add or drop certain aspects as needed. Therefore, the details change, the locations change, even the characters may change. That's how the organ harvesters were able to move so quickly from their New Orleans operation (yep, pun intended) to Las Vegas in different versions of the well-known horror tale.

WHAT IT LOOKS LIKE

Stories hold society together, helping us to stay connected despite differences in age, background, and worldview. Urban legends fill

1. Some purists require an urban legend to be an actual story with a cast or characters and a recognizable plot and therefore consider email virus hoaxes and odd facts or beliefs to be categorized as contemporary lore—but not actual urban legends. For our purposes, though, we're inaccurately referring to all contemporary folktales as urban legends. It's simpler that way. So there.

a particular niche by adhering to a handful of implied thematic elements—horror, humor, warning, embarrassment, and sympathy, to name a few—that reflect our shared concerns or beliefs.

The best urban legends contain more than one of these elements. Consider the classic "Surprise Party" story. I heard this one during my freshman year of college; the storyteller was a student from Southwestern Baptist Theological Seminary. According to her, this happened to an engaged couple one of her friends supposedly knew:

> Two seminary students met and fell in love during their first year at the seminary and had recently become engaged. They went out to dinner a few weeks after the engagement to celebrate her birthday. After dessert, they decided to stop by her parents' house for a sweater. No one was there, and—despite their chosen career paths—one premarital thing led to another. Long story short, they ended up naked and fooling around upstairs. Pretty soon the phone rang; it was the girl's mother. Mom wanted her to go downstairs and set the VCR for her favorite show. Still feeling playful (and still quite unclothed) the guy suggested a piggyback ride for his naked fiancée. She hopped onto his shoulders, he started down the stairs, and as the two of them reached the bottom, the lights clicked on. A host of people yelled, "Surprise!" The two naughty seminarians were surrounded by their best friends, fellow church members, and even the girl's parents. The engagement was eventually called off, and neither finished their religious education.

Upon first hearing this one, I believed it. Then I heard it again the next summer, from a different source. And in that retelling, the protagonists weren't from the seminary but were a recently married pastor and his wife. Coincidence? I began to have my doubts. Then I heard it again a couple of years ago, and this version starred a naked boyfriend and girlfriend who went into the basement to turn off the clothes dryer, where they were surprised by a party. Bingo. A quintessential urban legend, with all the standard elements.

"The Surprise Party" is a cautionary tale, one that uses its lurid details to teach us a moral lesson: that premarital hanky-panky has negative consequences. See what happens when you, um, count the chickens before they hatch? It's also got humor. What's funnier than a naked piggyback into a room full of your closest friends? It's got embarrassment. What's worse than a naked piggyback smack into the up-close-and-personal scrutiny of your future in-laws? And some versions of the story even include horror. In the final account I heard—the one with the boyfriend/girlfriend and the clothes dryer—the female ended up having a nervous breakdown.

Most urban legends contain one or more of these thematic touchstones. The best ones contain them all, tying everything together at the end with a you-won't-believe-it twist.

WHERE IT COMES FROM

An urban legend, very simply, comes from someone you know. While the story itself might be outlandish, the teller usually isn't. It's someone you trust, and she swears up and down that this really happened to her friend's uncle or to the receptionist at her dad's office or to somebody her neighbor knows. What reason do you have to doubt? Plenty.

Regardless of their storytelling prowess, no one wants to begin a good story with "... so I heard this from my friend Sean who heard it from his dentist who swears this happened to the friend of a cousin of an old Army buddy of his." That's way too bulky. Instead

we streamline the intro—"This happened to a guy Sean knows"—
giving the impression that we're only a step or two away from the
event itself, when actually we're hundreds or even thousands of
people removed. The surprise party story that supposedly happened
to someone my friend knew? It's been around since the 1920s.[2]

The problem is that we're gullible. We believe what we hear,
and urban legends hit the stuff we're already thinking about. We're
primed to believe them. That's why horror stories and cautionary
sex tales show up so often in urban legends. We fear disease, sexual
deviance, and public embarrassment. We worry about kidnappings,
gang violence, and contaminated food. We distrust the government
and large corporations. We're afraid of—evidently—kidney thieves.
In previous centuries, people were terrified of the deep, dark
woods (home to mysterious and dangerous creatures), and this
apprehension found its way into folk tales like "Little Red Riding
Hood" or "Hansel and Gretel."

WHERE IT'S GOING

Urban legends are today's fairy tales. But instead of telling each
other stories over the campfire or dinner table as we once did, we
now spread them via the click of the mouse. Contemporary folklore
can now reach thousands of "listeners" as fast as you can forward an
email or post on a blog. That's why folklore has flourished in the last
ten years like no other time in the history of the world. So does this
lead to a boom in creativity? A utopia of cultural understanding? A
swarm of excellent storytellers? Um … no. Instead it leads to a hard
drive stuffed full of virus hoaxes, faked photos, computer scams, and
useless petitions—crap we're far too willing to pass on with a click,
just in case it's true.

It's usually not.

---

2. This according to urban legend experts David and Barbara Mikkelson, who operate
the highly informative Urban Legend Reference Pages at *www.snopes.com*. For more on
the "Surprise Party" story, see *www.snopes.com/sex/caught/surpart1.htm*.

On one hand, our technology has made us all a lot more informed about our world. On the other hand, it's turned us into a bunch of easily fleeced forwarders of virus warnings.

So what's the answer? Do we dismiss every cautionary email as a hoax? Well, not exactly. Some are legitimate warnings, such as the mass-mailing Sober.N worm that made the rounds in early 2005 or the W32/VBSun-A virus that cleverly disguised itself as a tsunami disaster donation plea. But most of the others are phony, like *A (Virtual) Card for You, Life Is Beautiful.pps, It Takes Guts to Say Jesus.*

Here's the problem, though: Deciding to ignore every virus warning that comes across your desktop could be harmful. And knee-jerk forwarding can be annoying. The solution is simple. Do your homework. Check out the Computers section of the Urban Legends Reference Pages at Snopes.com, which regularly posts updates—along with "real vs. hoax" ratings—of the emails currently making the rounds. Another excellent resource is the Urban Legends and Folklore section at About.com. These sites can generally tell you whether a warning is real within a click or two.

FINAL WORDS

Don't be an email forwarder by any means. But if you encounter a too-good-to-be-true story? A tale of kidney-gutting horror or hook-handed killers or bodies under the bed? By all means, enjoy it. Embellish. Have fun. Make it your own. Say it really happened—*no, seriously, really!*—to your sister's tattooist or your mom's parole officer. Spin a clever yarn. Remember, by passing along an honest-to-goodness urban legend, you're contributing to a greater good. You're preserving our culture through oral tradition. Because if each of us fails to do our part, the generations to follow will grow up having never heard about Richard Gere and the gerbil.

And that, friends, would be truly shameful.

CHAPTER SIXTEEN

GENEROSITY IS A VIRTUE, AND HERE'S WHY

Are you ready? Because here comes the guilt trip. Despite the economic uncertainty of the last few years, the United States and its citizens are living in a period of remarkable prosperity. It's been estimated that Americans own nearly 40 percent of the world's wealth while comprising only 2.5 percent of the world's population. If you have enough food to eat, clothes to keep you warm, a roof over your head, and a car to get you places, then you can count yourself wealthier than 85 percent of the rest of humanity. You may be a cash-deprived grad student, a young professional just getting started, or a newlywed scraping by on a budget, but if you had the disposable income to buy this book (thanks for that, by the way), then you're rich, comparatively speaking.

So ... the question is, do you feel guilty yet?

Should you feel guilty?

Well, in a word: No. You can't help that you were born into Western culture and its abundance. It's not your fault that you probably come from a solid middle-class family, born during a prosperous period in the world's most prosperous country.

Don't feel guilty for being comfortable. Nope. Feel guilty when you refuse to *share* that comfort. Take it from a higher authority: "From everyone who has been given much, much will be demanded; and from the one who has been entrusted with much, much more will be asked."[1]

We've been given much. Compared to the rest of the world, we're the caretakers of power, wealth, privilege, and opportunity. Our responsibility, then, is to pass some of it around. To practice generosity, not as an occasional virtue but as a lifestyle. Work hard. Make money, and don't be ashamed of it. But when the time comes, share it. The best life is one of open-handed generosity.

GENEROSITY COMBATS MATERIALISM

It's not wrong to make money. It's not wrong to buy stuff with it. But there are a lot of needs in this world, and a second Lincoln Navigator is not necessarily one of them. The best way to fight our society's obsession with wealth and the toys it can buy us is to treat possessions like the fleeting extras they are. Materialism builds a shrine to the things we own. Generosity kicks the shrine over and gives away the parts.

There are a number of practices that merge generosity with an antimaterialistic bent. Here are some examples:

Giving away your money. This one's so obvious, but here it is anyway: from churches to children's charities to AIDS relief in

1. Luke 14:48 (New International Version).

Africa, nothing goes further than a good old American dollar. There are as many organizations out there as stars in the sky, but not all of them have the same twinkle. Before writing your check, do your homework. Find out how much of your donation actually goes to the cause. Some foundations give 100 percent to people in need. Others have heady operating costs, which they're required to divulge. Ask questions. Then, once you've found a charity with which you're comfortable, start sharing.

Giving away your extra stuff. All of us have closets packed with clothing we haven't worn for years. Maybe we're hoping our parachute pants will someday be stylish again. Or, more likely, we just grew bored with the perfectly fine wardrobe we had and bought something else. But if you don't wear it, why keep it? Yes, you could sell it on eBay or in a consignment store, but that would be so predictable. Instead, give it away. Whether you have excess clothing, books, musical instruments, tools, or toys, chances are good that someone else would be ecstatic to have it.

Sharing the stuff you keep. When our two kids were born, my wife and I experienced generosity on a firsthand basis. It began with our headfirst tumble into the cash-burning world of baby supplies. As far as human lives go, there is no more expensive time than Year Zero through Year Two. Diapers, formula, baby food—all expensive, all useful for about five minutes. Same goes for the clothing. We were saved countless times by our family and friends, who willingly loaned us boxes full of baby clothing. They had the right idea: Is it better for this outfit to hang in a closet somewhere or to be put to use on a child? The same applies to maternity clothing, old computer systems, tools, even vehicles. Make your stuff available to others, and it'll naturally become less important to you (especially when, as often occurs, you don't get it back).

GENEROSITY EXTENDS YOUR INFLUENCE

Here's a personal story. My paternal grandparents lived frugally and saved a lot of money. Each of them took large portions of their wages in company stock, hoping one day to better the lives of their children and grandchildren. They've been successful.

My brother, my sister, my three cousins, and myself have all benefited from my grandparents' humble generosity. They have periodically withdrawn from their stock holdings to help send us grandkids to college, paying for books, tuition, room and board—even making loans to us for our first cars. Once we moved into the working world, they insisted upon using their savings to help us make decent down payments on our first homes. "What would we do with it?" my grandmother always asks. "Go to Vegas?"

That's generosity, and we'd all do a lot worse than to follow their example. My grandparents have led a simple life. They live in a modest home, drive a practical car, attend an average-sized church. She was a bank teller, he a decorated World War II veteran and refinery worker. Yet portraits of their generosity are painted daily by the lives they helped shape—among them, a poet, an inner-city minister, businessmen, a beloved teacher, a doting father of twins, a writer. All my grandparents wanted to do was to help us out, but they ended up making us who we are.

A lifestyle of giving meets immediate needs, but it also lays a foundation for the future. And by way of that foundation, one's life grows exponentially, extending into future generations. Sharing makes you bigger than you are. My grandparents hit eighty a few years ago. Things are slowing down. And though they may not be around a whole lot longer, their legacy certainly will.

GENEROSITY CHALLENGES SELFISHNESS

I'm self-involved, you're self-involved, and both of us know it. There's nothing explicitly wrong with that, because being concerned with our own interests is the only way to protect our well-being. We're self-centered because it's practical, and it's necessary in order to live a fulfilling, productive life. But when such a mindset begins to exalt our own well-being at the expense of someone else's, then it turns into the bad kind of selfishness, the kind that takes advantage of people—or completely ignores them—to satisfy personal needs. Grabbing an umbrella when it begins to rain? That's an acceptable self-centeredness. But grabbing an umbrella out of an old lady's hand? That's the bad kind.

Our problem is that it's really easy to slide from Point A (self-protection) to Point B (self-protection at poor old Ethel's expense). Like trying to brake on an icy road, sometimes the momentum carries us too far.

There's a Zen story about a time when the Japanese master Nan-in met with a university professor who came to inquire about the religion. Nan-in, always a gracious host, served tea to his visitor. He poured until the professor's cup was full but didn't stop there. He kept pouring and pouring. The hot tea went everywhere, sloshing over the sides and onto the table. The professor watched in disbelief until he couldn't help himself. "That's enough!" he said. "The cup is full. No more will go in." Nan-in smiled and said, "You are the same. Like this cup, you are full of opinions and speculations. How can I show you Zen unless you first empty your cup?"[2]

Day in and day out, our lives are being filled with the stuff of self. We work for personal fulfillment. We work to make money. The fulfillment gives our lives meaning, and the money supports our lifestyles. We make decisions based on our personal goals. We pursue leisure to provide balance. We rest in order to recharge. All of these are necessary, but guess what? They all focus inward. By merely going through the motions of living, we're constantly filling our cups with self. Again, not wrong—just the way we're made. But the more self we put in, the less room there is for the truly important stuff. These are the virtues of selflessness—love, compassion, understanding—and a responsible, full adult life ought to make room for them. Generosity of time, money, and possessions is a way of emptying our cup, of making space. The more we pour out, the more life will be able to pour back in.

FINAL WORDS

We've been thinking primarily about generosity as it relates to possessions and money, but don't forget that one of the most valuable commodities in today's society is time. Volunteerism, simply, is being generous with your time, and it's just as valid a form of giving—it, too, is a way to "empty the cup." If you can't afford to help financially, help in other ways.

True, selfless giving remains one of our loftiest aims. It makes us richer than money or possessions ever could. Like any habit, it needs to be cultivated, but the yield is remarkable. Start the habit of sharing now, whether it's your time, your money, or your stuff. You won't regret it.

CHAPTER SEVENTEEN

HOW TO PLAY POKER LIKE AN HONEST-TO-GOODNESS CELEBRITY

Apparently, poker is a fairly popular game. Just a few years ago, it was no more than a smoky garage diversion for American males or a seedy casino fixture that no one understood. Then television discovered it.

And before you could say *Celebrity Poker Showdown*, the game had become a national phenomenon. It's not surprising. Poker blends chance and skill, confidence and competition into a social activity unmatched by most other pastimes. Sure, you can watch it on TV, but you can also play at home with your friends, and the resulting combo of low-end wagering, friendly atmosphere, and limitless game variations guarantees a fun evening, with or without the beer (which, Lesson Number One, is often not the best beverage to consume when gambling).

In a society where everyone from demure housewives to television stars are throwing around phrases like "he tried to squeeze out a diamond flush on the river but turned up short," hip adults need to have a basic understanding of the game. If poker's popularity has left you behind, here's a chance to get dealt back in.

THE BASICS

Poker is played with a full deck of fifty-two cards, ranked from Ace to Ace. At its most basic version the game is played with each player being dealt five cards; whoever holds the highest cards at the end wins. From low to high, the hierarchy is: Ace, Two, Three, Four, Five, Six, Seven, Eight, Nine, Ten, Jack, Queen, King, Ace. The ace can be either high or low depending on the hand, but *never* both in the same hand.

Poker is a democratic game. Suits (Clubs, Diamonds, Hearts, Spades) matter on some occasions, but none is considered higher than another.

WHAT BEATS WHAT

How do you determine who has the highest hand? Simple. Follow the hierarchy. Knowing this sequence is one of the best steps you can take toward understanding the game. After all, if you don't know what's supposed to happen after everyone displays their cards, you might as well go back to Solitaire. Here's the list from top to bottom:

ROYAL FLUSH: The five highest cards of the same suit (Ace, King, Queen, Jack, Ten). This is the Holy Grail of poker—it can't be beaten in a non-wild-card game. Odds of being dealt this hand in five cards are 1 in 650,000. So if you get it twice in a row, you're probably cheating.

STRAIGHT FLUSH: Same as above (a royal flush *is* a straight flush), but it doesn't have to be face cards. An Ace can be high or low; wraparound is not allowed (i.e. King, Ace, Two, Three, Four). A straight is no royal flush, but it's still impressive.

FOUR OF A KIND: Four cards with the same number or face ranking. Someone would need to have an unbelievable hand to take on a Four, so bet on it.

FULL HOUSE: Three cards of a kind combined with a pair. Still a great hand, but there's always a chance someone else will also have a full house. If this occurs, the tiebreaker goes to whomever has the higher-ranking triplet.

FLUSH: Here's where suit matters. A flush is any five non-consecutive cards of the same suit. Make sure you're matching suit and not just color (for example, mixing in a diamond among a four-card flush of hearts). You'll be mocked. Then you'll lose your money.

STRAIGHT: A straight of cards, as above, only this time they don't have to be the same suit. Ace can be high or low, and no wraparound allowed. The straight with the highest card wins the tiebreaker.

THREE OF A KIND: Three cards of any rank (plus two more non-matching cards). Highest three of a kind wins in the event of a tie.

TWO PAIR: See where we're going with this? High pair wins in a tie.

ONE PAIR: Loser.

HIGH CARD: The person holding the highest card when no one else has absolutely anything.

THE MOST POPULAR VARIATIONS

FIVE-CARD DRAW: The basic game. Deal five cards face-down to each player. There is an initial betting round, then each player is allowed to trade one, two, or three cards with the deck (three is the max). Another betting round follows. Keep reading if you're not sure what "betting round" means.

FIVE-CARD STUD: The basic game, but with a cool-sounding name and a twist. Dealing sequence can vary, but it usually provides each player with two cards face-down on the table and three cards, eventually, face-up (five cards total). The betting round begins with the high hand after the first three cards have been dealt (two down, one up). Then, another card is dealt, followed by another betting round. Repeat for final card.

SEVEN-CARD STUD: Same as above, only using seven cards in a combination of three down, four up. Winner has the best hand using the five best cards out of his or her seven.

LOWBALL: Five cards are dealt to each player following the rules of Five-Card Draw—except this time, you're trying for the worst hand. A good game to suggest when you find yourself folding every other deal.

TEXAS HOLD'EM: This is the game played by the poker deities at high-stakes venues and what you'll usually be treated to when watching the game on TV. It's world-series stuff and can be pretty complex for a beginner, so be cautious when it's suggested. Deal two cards face-down to each player (these are called "Hole" or "Pocket" cards). A round of betting commences (often a blind bet, made before seeing your cards—again, serious stuff). Then, three cards are dealt face-up in the middle of the table. This is called the "flop." Don't ask why. There is a round of betting, based on your two pocket cards and the three flop cards. Another card is added to the flop (this one's called the "turn"). Another round of betting. Finally, a fifth card (the "river"), and a final round of betting. You make your best hand based on your two pocket cards and any three cards in the community flop. In casinos, this can be a very expensive game, with the pot doubling or tripling on the turn and river bets.

HOW THE BETTING WORKS

After the dealer announces which version of the game is to be played—but before the cards are dealt—all players must "ante up" by placing the minimum table bet (the "ante") into the pot. This predetermined amount ensures that everyone playing has some stake in the game. By not anteing, you either indicate that you don't understand the game being played or you aren't participating in this round. Or you're flat out of money, which indicates you should have left about an hour ago.

The player to the left of the dealer typically opens the betting (though he may "check," or pass that privilege to the next player, if he chooses). After the betting is opened—let's say with a dime—it then moves to the next person at the table to continue. This person has three options. She can:

See the bet and call, which at the start of the game means matching the amount of the previous bet. In the example above, the player would wager a dime since the game and betting have just begun. In the next betting round, she'll need to meet the amount the bet has been raised since her most recent wager. If it raises at any point before returning to her, she'll have to calculate and pay that amount.

Raise the bet, meaning she not only matches the previous bet, but adds to it. In this example, she would see the bet with a dime and raise it a nickel. This makes it more expensive for others to remain in the game. There is typically a limit to the amount you can raise a bet.

Fold, like a paper airplane in the grubby hands of a nine-year-old. If you have a lousy hand, folding lets you out of the game. You forfeit the chance to win the pot, but you don't have to worry about losing any more than your ante. To fold, simply place your cards face-down on the table, and say, "I fold." Add a measure of disgust to your voice, and you might get sympathy.

Betting keeps everyone honest by increasing the pot while preventing players with bad hands from winning. Generally, those players who participate in the betting process are reasonably confident they have a chance to come out on top. Unless, of course, they're bluffing—which is basically a nice way to say "lying" when your cards suck but you want to make other players believe you're sporting a high hand. The bluffing player's only hope is that an initial high bet scares everyone off. Unless you're really, really good at poker, this probably won't work. Besides, no one likes a liar.

The only way to stay in a game is not to fold, so if you're ever going to win the pot in poker, you'll need to understand how and when to bet. If you have a bad hand, you should fold. If you have the makings of a good hand, just needing to replace one or two cards, then you should consider staying in. If you were just dealt a full house or a straight flush or four Kings, you should definitely stay in. Just don't start giggling or bouncing in your chair or giving some other signal that you're sitting on a sure thing.[1] If the rest of the players pick up on this, they'll fold, and all you'll get with your once-in-a-blue-moon hand is the ante. Play it cool, raise the betting with restraint, and see what happens.

The wagering aspect of poker—when to bet, how much to bet,

---

1. This inadvertent mannerism—a subtle physical clue that you have a good hand—is called a "tell," and experienced poker players learn to watch for them while hiding tells of their own. The trick is to be as stone-faced as possible when appraising your cards. Unless, of course, you're jittery all the time, in which case a serene, emotionless poker face would be so abnormal as to indicate something's up. Yep, tells can be tricky.

and how to increase the pot without practically saying, "Lookee! I've got a full house!"—isn't the kind of thing that's easily explained in a short chapter in a pocket-sized book. The fact is, you're gonna have to learn by playing. Find some buddies who know the game but are nice enough not to take advantage of your ignorance, and play. Keep it low-stakes, or no stakes at all. When I was a kid, my cousins and I used to play poker while betting with Skittles candies. Reds were the ante. We thought we were pretty cool.

(Turns out we were wrong.)

FINAL WORDS

Poker can be a fun game, and it's even more fun when you add a little money into the mix. It doesn't have to be much—a nickel, dime, or quarter ante is a great place to start. In fact, if the stakes are higher than that, lots of people won't play. High-stakes poker is much more stressful and, therefore, much less fun. The best advice when playing poker? Keep it light, loose, and social.

CHAPTER EIGHTEEN

STAYING IN SHAPE IS EASIER THAN YOU THINK, TUBBY

NEWSFLASH: Exercise is good for you.

And it's more than just a defensive strategy to keep your arms from flabbing and your gut from sagging. Regular exercise can benefit you as much as a balanced diet or regular checkups at the doctor. It reduces the risk of heart disease by improving blood circulation throughout the body. It lowers cholesterol levels, manages high blood pressure, and prevents bone loss. Exercise boosts your energy and releases tension. It improves your self-image, results in a better night's sleep, and helps fight anxiety and depression.

We all should exercise a bit more.

The snag is that, for many of us, a lifestyle of fitness seems inaccessible due to time, money, or physical constraints. Why? Because the act of staying in shape has gotten wrapped up with the health club culture. We associate "getting exercise" with going to the gym, wearing fancy workout clothes, strapping into a space-age weight-training machine, or signing up for classes full of sexy, 1-percent-body-fat, pneumatically gifted Energizer bunnies. In such environments, the intimidation level runs nearly as high as the bunnies' energy levels—and nothing will knock the legs out from under an exercise routine like the mistaken belief that you need to look like Angelina Jolie to be considered healthy.

The good news is that you don't have to sign up for expensive gym memberships to stay in shape. You can do it all by yourself, with no expensive equipment, no embarrassing clothing, and no glistening hardbodies nearby to mock your tonelessness. Here's something every adult should know: Keeping fit is much easier than you think. All it takes is a little creativity and determination.

GYMS ARE FOR SISSIES

Okay, that's not comprehensively true. There are tons of people who have found fitness clubs to be very beneficial. Clubs provide access to equipment and programs most of us don't have at home. And clubs boost productivity through social motivation—getting to the end of an AbBlast session in a class of twenty is loads easier than completing it by yourself at home.

But there's something odd about those shimmering bodies chugging away on those treadmills and bicycles. Because how many people do you know who will drive two miles to the health club, at which point they climb onto the treadmill for a two-mile jog? Or hoist themselves onto the exercise bike for several minutes of nondestination pedaling? Maybe there's something to be said for watching *CSI* while striding upon an eternal slab of rubber, but wouldn't it be just as beneficial to actually walk or run *to* the gym, where you could then participate in some other health-related activity? Or to cut out the expensive membership altogether and just go out and exercise in the real world?

Fresh morning air. Well-manicured lawns. Even busy city streets with countless things to see. Jogging outdoors is an adventure. Jogging on a treadmill is, well, not much different from a hamster wheel. Same goes for cycling. And what about the people who ride the elevator at work, then go to the gym for a stint on the stair stepper at the end of the day?

Here's the point: We are surrounded by opportunities to stay fit throughout the day, but because we're conditioned to associate exercise with the health club, we're blind to them. We're due for a redefinition of "exercise."

MOVE, BABY, MOVE

Exercising at the gym requires both time and money. Some of us don't have the time to commit to a daily or weekly gym routine. Others don't have the cash to join a club, which can begin at a basic $40 a month and grow from there. These things become prohibitive to people who'd like to exercise but just can't make the commitment. Fortunately for you, there's a simple solution to this problem: change your definition of exercise.

When most people think of exercise, they probably picture one of the following activities: weightlifting; a bouncy, cardio-intensive group workout like kickboxing or cardio-funk or salsa dancing; recreational sports like basketball or volleyball; a formal regimen of solo activity such as jogging, walking, or biking.

We can do better than that. How? By making exercise less formal. Instead of confining it to the examples above, let's identify exercise by one all-important attribute: movement. Exercise employs some form of movement toward the task of maintaining fitness. It means pumping your legs and flailing your arms, and doing so at a pace that gets your heart beating a little faster. Mix in some good arm and leg movement on a daily basis, and you've got yourself a gym-free lifestyle of fitness.

Consider housework. The simple activity of operating a vacuum cleaner requires movement. It's work. Next weekend, how about burning calories and boosting your heart rate by vacuuming with vigor? Put a little drive into your dusting. Scrub the tub with enthusiasm. Mow the yard, pull weeds, dig up the flower bed with gusto—intense gardening can burn as many calories as some health club activities. By adding a little energy and extra movement to your Saturday routine, you can turn a necessary, mundane task into an opportunity for exercise.

Sound too easy? Maybe so, but that's the beauty of the Movement Plan—it eases fitness into your busy lifestyle by locating it in unexpected places. One of the best ways to put it to work requires undergoing a simple mindset reversal, which is to ...

REJECT CONVENIENCE

Ours is a culture that wants convenience and wants it, like, right now. Or sooner, if you can swing that. We expect express lanes at the supermarket, express oil changes at the quick lube, and express credit card processing online. We clamor for drive-up pharmacies, drive-up coffee shops, and drive-up dry cleaners. We'll spend ten minutes circling a parking lot for a more convenient parking space, never realizing that had we parked as far away from the store as possible at the beginning and simply *started walking*, we'd be inside by now.

Every time we opt for convenience, we pass up a chance to exercise. The next time you go to work or the mall, pay attention to the way you do things. Make every decision as you normally would, but be aware of the missed opportunities. Do you take the elevator to your fourth-floor office instead of using the stairs? Do you make a phone call or dash off an email to a coworker when you could just as easily walk down the hall and talk in person? Do you ride the escalator from one floor to the next at the mall, staring past the hardy souls shlepping their shopping bags up the adjoining staircase? Do you contentedly watch children running and playing at the park, or do you actually run and play *with* them?

Rebelling against a life of ease is one way to exploit the many chances for fitness we encounter every day. But if you absolutely *have* to ride the elevator, you might consider another option, which is to ...

GET OUT AND WALK

In a 2002 survey conducted by RT Neilson for Recreational Equipment, Inc. (REI), the popular specialty outdoors retail chain, more than 70 percent of Americans said that outdoor leisure activities are more effective in relieving stress than indoor ones. Nine out of ten respondents indicated that spending time outside lifted their spirits.[1] Going outside is good for you.

So do you have to mountain bike, snowshoe, or kayak to exercise outdoors? Nope. Although those activities do carry something of a cool quotient, they can be just as expensive as a gym membership. A more reasonable idea is just to go outside and walk. According to the National Institute of Health and the Dietary Guidelines

---

1. "Small Tracts," *Common Ground: Conservation News from the Conservation Fund* (January–March 2002) p. 4.

Advisory Committee, thirty minutes of light activity every day is enough exercise for the average person.[2] Why not make that thirty minutes of outdoor walking?

Perhaps you think you're too busy to find that kind of time, but you're wrong. Consider your workday. Many working Joes take a couple of fifteen-minute breaks during the day, one in the morning and one in the afternoon. Add that to a half-hour- or hour-long lunch break, and you've got plenty of time during the day to get moving. Instead of hanging out by the coffee machine or browsing eBay during your breaks, why not get some fresh air? Walk around the block a few times. Explore the neighborhood around your office. At lunch, pick a restaurant ten minutes from the office and walk there and back. Keep a steady pace. If the weather gets bad, walk up and down the halls or climb staircases.

FINAL WORDS

Fitting physical activities into your daily routine does wonders for your lifestyle. It refreshes your spirits, burns calories, and increases your energy level. You look better, feel better, and perform better. Be aware of how lazy you've become—how lazy we've *all* become— then do something about it. Change your habits, defy convenience, thumb your nose at our too-efficient society.

There's nothing wrong with going to the gym, of course. If you can afford the time and the expense, then by all means make it a part of your day. Good for you. But for those of us who can't, we have to find our own way to stay in shape. Luckily, these opportunities are right in front of us.

2. Eugenia Halsey, "Government's New Advice: Exercise Every Day," CNN.com (posted January 2, 1996, at *www.cnn.com/HEALTH/9601/dietary_guidelines*).

19

FINANCIAL PROCRASTINATION WILL EAT YOU FOR LUNCH

Almost all of us have had to deal with some form of procrastination over the years. Waiting until the last minute to begin research papers. Earning fines because we can't seem to find the time to return that rented *Goonies* DVD. Getting the car inspected in May when the sticker expired in February. Filing our taxes.

Oooooh—taxes. Let's stop right there.

For most of us, long-delayed school assignments are in the past. An overdue inspection sticker, while technically against the law, is only a big deal if you get pulled over. And who doesn't have time to watch another round of *Goonies*? (Put your hands down.) That kind of procrastinating—while not exactly responsible—is relatively harmless. Live and learn, right?

But the *financial* kind of procrastination? That's something entirely different. Waiting too long to make good financial choices can screw you over for years to come. Financial procrastination is a big deal—a big, fat, expensive deal.

So here's a big, fat nugget of wisdom: When it comes to finances, *do not* postpone the big decisions just because you're still young and carefree. Why? Because you're likely to end up old and poor.

DEVELOP A BUDGET

Without a budget—a dedicated spending plan—people end up buying stuff and paying bills willy-nilly. The money goes to whatever they want ("It was on sale! It would be sinful not to buy it!"), with the leftovers applied toward the necessities. That's fun at first: no stress, lots of stuff. Who wouldn't benefit from an extra ski jacket, anyway? Unfortunately, this "system" can bottom out quickly, and you reach the point where there's no money left to pay the bills (fortunately for you, you'll have all those ski jackets to wear after the gas company turns off your heat). By then it's too late. You resort to credit cards, fall prey to the minimum monthly payments, wince as the interest kicks in, and suddenly the wide road toward debt stretches before you like a desolate highway.

Learning to live on a budget is something many discover a bounced check or a bankruptcy too late. It requires discipline and planning. It means giving up the impulse-buy high that consumers thrive on. But if money is consistently tight and bill payments are consistently late, there's no more important step to take financially. Make a plan while you're young, stick to it religiously, and life will be easier.

Start by listing all your expenses during an average month. This includes basic needs (rent, food, car, insurance, utilities, etc.) as well as unexpected or irregular expenditures like visits to the dentist or household repairs. It also includes retirement savings. If you want, you can even figure in an amount for frivolous stuff like shoe sales at the mall, movies, extra cheese on your burritos—whatever makes you happy. Add those up, then compare them with your monthly cash flow. Take into account every penny you'll make from stable sources of income, including salary, part-time wages, interest from a savings account, cash from Grandma, and anything else that's dependable month to month. Don't consider irregular sources of income such as bonuses, overtime pay, or birthday gifts. Then compare your two lists: net expenditures versus net income.

Let's say your net expenditures for each month are $2,500. Your monthly take-home income is $3,000. For the budget-conscious, that means all but $500 each month is designated toward something specific. The rest is "free" spending money. So does that mean you can go and blow it on Ding Dongs and Yoo-hoo? Not necessarily. The best course of action is to save as much of it as you can—everyone should have some emergency money stashed away in an easily accessed savings account, just in case. That way, you're never floored by the unexpected, like a car wreck, a hard drive failure, or even a layoff.

Finally, once you've set your budget, stick to it. Get it through your brain that when an amount of money is designated toward a regular expenditure, *it's gone.* The cash may still be in your checking account, but you can't touch it. That's the one rule to budgeting: Don't flex when it comes to concrete items. It may be okay to draw from your entertainment or clothing budget to cover an unforeseen expense, but you cannot steal from the money set aside for rent just because FunJet is offering a special to Cozumel.

So start planning your spending now. Make it routine. It may be a little painful at first, but like any habit, you'll quickly get to where you don't even notice it. Without a budget, you spend too much, buy stuff you don't need, and put yourself at risk. With a budget, you get your bills paid on time, you increase your savings, and you even have something left over at the end of the month—something *besides* a stack of past-due bills.

PLANNING FOR RETIREMENT

For most of us, retirement is in the neighborhood of forty years away. That's way too far into the future to even consider, right? Why sock away $100 a month when those dollars could be spent on, say, the new MP3 player/microbrowser/meat thermometer that everyone at work is packing? Or why save something you won't use for decades when you're not even sure you can make next month's mortgage payment?

We can always come up with reasons not to do something. Lack of time. Lack of ability. Lack of understanding. But in the case of retirement planning, every month you procrastinate costs you big time. That hundred dollars you can't afford to save this month? Forty years from now, that's $5,000.

Big difference.

This is explained in greater detail in chapter 14, but it's worth going over again. Why? Because you need to understand—today, while you're young—the value of compounded interest and how it works in saving for retirement. Let's say you sell your collection of Boba Fett paraphernalia on eBay and net $10,000 from it (nice collection, dork). You decide to forgo the new gadgets and invest the money instead. Very smart. If you invest that ten grand at the age of thirty-five and average 10 percent interest, you'll see that sum grow to $175,000 by the time you're sixty-five.[1] That's good money.

---

1. Unless you're reading this in 1997 via time travel or something, getting 10 percent interest is a pipe dream. But indulge me here—it's a good round number.

But what if you made the same investment ten years earlier? Take the original $10,000 and invest it at twenty-five instead of thirty-five. Multiply it by the same interest, only this time you're giving it ten extra years to grow. By the time you're sixty-five, you'll have more than $450,000 in the bank. That's nearly an extra three hundred grand, just for starting earlier.

If *time = money*, then *procrastination = lots less money*.

Don't put off saving for retirement any longer. If your company offers a 401(k), contribute as much as you can. If not, set up a regular or Roth IRA and start saving. Every little bit counts. Regardless of the monthly contribution or even the interest rate, you'll do tons better by starting now than if you wait a few more years or even months. Put time on your side.

PAYING OFF DEBT

It happens to everybody. Sometimes credit cards and uncontrolled spending are the culprits. Maybe it's car trouble or a medical emergency. In many cases, it's school loans. Everyone carries a little bit of debt. Most financial experts even recommend it, in the form of a mortgage, when it comes to home ownership. But for some people, debt can get out of hand. A couple of missed Visa payments, a home improvement loan, a blown transmission. And before you know it, a few hundred dollars of debt have ballooned into a few thousand.

Not good.

The easiest way to fall into debt is to live above your means via the improper use of credit cards. The temptation is powerful: Buy what you want, whip out the Platinum, and make the minimum payment until you can find the funds to cover it. No harm, no foul—until you consider that, after subtracting your minimum payment, the balance of your credit card account is subjected to exorbitant interest in the realm of 18, 19, even 20 percent and above. Here's the really scary part. Throw a few hundred bucks on the card, start making minimum payments, and you'll never—*never*—pay the card off. Give it a few years of unhindered growth, and it'll reach monster proportions. It'll wreck your credit history. And bad credit history hangs around a long, long time.

So if you've amassed any non-mortgage debt at all, most experts will tell you paying it down should be your primary goal. People often procrastinate because a task or project seems too overwhelming to even think about tackling. If that's the case, take a few small steps. Select your smallest debt (maybe a gas card account) and get it paid off first. When that's done, move on to the next one. Save money. Sell stuff you don't need. Compare prices. Any extra you have each month goes to debt payment.

FINAL WORDS

Procrastination is a guaranteed way to lose money, whether it's the retirement savings you missed out on or the debt you let yourself slip into. It's tempting to pass off these worries as irrelevant to someone at your stage of life—retirement is for old people, budgeting is for accountants and dads—but don't give in. Start now, and save yourself the trouble. Financial freedom starts with discipline, but it ends with peace. And long, restful nights. And light-blue belted jumpsuits, but maybe that's just my granddad.

20

MYSTERY DUMPLINGS AND THE KEY TO LASTING RELATIONSHIPS

There's a weird-looking mountain on the outskirts of Kaohsiung in southern Taiwan. The mountain is named *Ban Pin Shan*—literally, "half-faced mountain." It looks like the leftover crown of a half-eaten cupcake, bit right through the top. You're about to find out how it got that name.

Years ago, the mountain was still whole, and a small fishing village lay in its foothills. One day, an elderly stranger entered the village. His long hair and beard were white, his clothes ragged and torn. He brought with him a crate full of hot dumplings. Their delicious aroma could be smelled throughout the village, and a crowd soon gathered around him.

"Hot and delicious dumplings!" the man shouted. "One for ten cents, two for twenty cents, three for free!"

The crowd murmured. Three for free? No one did business that way. Old guy must be insane. But he kept at it. "Dumplings! One for ten, two for twenty, three for free!"

As the story goes, a villager with the unfortunate name of BigHead Wang was the first to take up the strange old man on his offer. "I'll find out whether they're really free," Wang said. He stepped up and ordered three steaming dumplings. His face lit up as he popped the first, big as a chicken's egg, into his mouth. Best thing he'd ever eaten. He devoured the second dumpling, but quickly grew so full he could hardly think about eating more.

The old man stretched out an open palm. "Twenty cents," he said.

Wang swallowed. "If I eat three dumplings, I don't have to pay, right?"

The old man assured him that three dumplings were indeed free. So Wang stuffed one final dumpling into his mouth. The stranger kept his word and didn't charge BigHead Wang a cent. The deal was legit. The villagers went crazy; men and women began ordering and eating dumplings as fast as possible. Everyone received three free dumplings—no one ordered just one or two—until the crate was empty. The old man smiled and left. Those who hadn't received a dumpling were utterly disappointed.

That evening and the next morning, word spread about the crazy dumpling man. "Who is this guy?" villagers asked. "Where did he come from?"

He returned the second day. "Hot and delicious dumplings!" he shouted. "One for ten cents, two for twenty, three for free!" A near riot ensued, and the crate emptied within minutes.

The scene repeated on day three. Villagers surrounded the feeble old man like wolves on a wounded deer, grasping at the prized dumplings, until finally a single voice rose out of the crowd. "Mister?" a young man said. "I'd like only one dumpling. Just one, please."

The frenzy came to a standstill. "Wait," said the old man. "Did you hear me clearly? I said 'three for free.' Why are you just asking for one?"

The young man fidgeted. "I feel bad for you," he said. "You've carried this huge load of dumplings to us every day, and we've enjoyed them so much. But you've not made any money yet. I'd like to pay. Please give me only one dumpling." The gluttonous villagers backed away, hanging their heads in shame.

The old man laughed. "At last," he said, "I have found you! You, young man, are the only person in this village suitable to be my pupil."

This astonished the crowd. "Dumpling man, who are you?" BigHead Wang asked, licking his gooey fingers.

The old man pointed. "I am the god from behind that mountain." As the villagers turned their heads, they noticed that half the mountain was missing—a huge chunk was gone, as if it had been sliced away by a giant knife. The horrible truth dawned on them, and the crowd rushed back to the crate. Where the dumplings had been, there was only black, oozing mud. The mountain god had fed them the soil of the mountain itself.

The kindhearted young man soon departed with the deity to learn the ways of magic. And the villagers wept, sick and disgusted at their selfishness. They named the mountain *Ban Pin Shan*—"half-faced mountain"—and would forever remember their greed toward the gifts of the mountain god.[1]

---

1. I first encountered the legend of Ban Pin Shan at the Folk Stories of Taiwan Web Site: *www.taiwandc.org/folk-ban.htm*. And, yep, BigHead Wang really is the guy's name. And, no, he's not in the porn industry.

WHAT YOU DO WITH THE DUMPLINGS

Ask anyone who's been married for a significant period of time. Ask anyone in a well-adjusted and generally happy family. Ask longtime friends, longtime coworkers, longtime business partners. How do you sustain a good relationship for so long? How do you keep from driving each other crazy? From not letting occasional blowups completely devour the relationship?

You'll probably get some variation of the same answer: Get over yourself. Think of the other person first. Forget about your own needs once in a while. Be considerate and thoughtful. Cooperate, work together, practice selflessness.

What's the secret to a lasting relationship? Self-sacrifice. And not just on one side; it applies to both members of any relationship. Married couples need to shed selfishness like wedding clothes in a honeymoon suite. Friends have to meet each other's needs for companionship. Business partners have to work together for the good of the business. Family members have to put aside their personal agendas in order to keep the peace.

Self-sacrifice is the key. And it's a relatively simple concept, one that basically comes down to just one thing: what you do with the dumplings.

"Finally," you're thinking. "I was wondering how that convoluted story applied to anything." To which I reply: *shut up*. It's a clever allegory and an interesting folktale, and besides, it involves a character named BigHead Wang. Which is awesome.

Relationships are hard. Sharing your life with another person is no run through a sun-dappled wheat field. What usually trips us up is the "sharing" part, because when we enter into any relationship, we expect dumplings. (The figurative kind.) We usually decide to date someone, befriend someone, and partner with someone in business based on what we might gain from them—excitement, confidence, companionship, comfort, support, success. But rarely do we think about what we might be able to *give*.

HOW TO NOT BE SUCH A SELFISH LOUT

Our self-centeredness is natural. You don't have to teach little kids to look out for themselves. It's part of the survival/self-preservation package we were all born with. Still, each of us has the capacity for moving toward the opposite mindset, especially in the relationships with the people who matter most to us. And "moving toward" that goal is a deliberate choice of words, because true selflessness is a destination none of us will probably ever reach. The pursuit, however, is worthwhile and makes the race so much better. Here are a few small steps to take daily to get closer to the goal.

Practice politeness. Basic manners are gradually falling away in our society, which is unfortunate, because the whole point behind politeness is showing respect for other people. Dedicate yourself to reversing that trend. Open doors for people—women, men, children, the elderly, people you know, people you don't know, people who look at you suspiciously while you're doing it. Give up your seat on the bus or subway when someone else needs it. Smile and look people in the eye. Politeness in your public life is one of those things that oozes over into your private life. If you can be polite to strangers, you can be polite in the relationships that count.

Listen more than you speak. Some of us can't keep our mouths shut. We can't wait for the other person to finish talking so we can get in the last word. So we can turn the conversation back toward ourselves. Selflessness caps off that bubbling verbal fountain and listens first. It waits for another person to finish talking before jumping in with our comments or anecdotes or opinions. Because failing to do so? Gives the not-so-subtle hint that what we have to say is way more important than what our companion has to say. Step off the ego train and listen.

When you do speak, speak gracefully. This seems rudimentary—honestly, it's kindergarten stuff—but that's because Miss Manners hasn't had any clout in our society for years. We're so used to dashing off quick emails and IMs where efficiency is the rule, and only the most essential words get used. And that clipped form of digital communication is slowly trickling into our flesh-and-blood interaction. It's cold. Gracious speech warms it back up. Make it a point to say "please" more often. Say "thank you." Apologize when you bump into someone or step on a toe at the movie theater. Get someone's attention by saying "excuse me" rather than "Hey!" When you meet someone, make sure you offer some sort of "nice to meet you" acknowledgment. And liberally hand out compliments to the people you know.[2]

Serve. This is *so* against the grain but a huge step toward healthy relationships. Be a servant. Get up off your butt and do a little work for the other person. Be the one to replenish your spouse's coffee at breakfast. Jump up and wash the dishes after the family meal. Volunteer to help a friend move before he or she asks. Always offer to help—at work, at home, at play. Stop taking. Start giving.

Be generous. This is covered in full in Chapter 16, but loosen your grip on your time, money, and stuff—especially within the key relationships in your life. This goes without saying in a marriage, but it also applies to friends and family. Share and try not to worry about whether your generosity gets returned.

Change yourself first. Anytime a problem creeps up in a relationship, our first instinct is to blame the other person. Selflessness, however, dictates that we work to transform ourselves

---

2. But just the people you know. Liberally handing out comments to strangers—"Lady, you don't know me, but you're lookin' hot in those jeans!"—is rarely acceptable.

first. And guess what? It's easier to change yourself than someone else.

FINAL WORDS

Some people are fantastic givers. They share and share and share, and their dumplings always seem to magically replenish. So their spouses, partners, and friends get into the habit of taking and taking and taking, and the relationship seems to work. For a while. The dumplings are yummy, right? And they always show up again the next day. But at some point, the dumplings will be gone, and nothing will have ever been paid. What then?

Don't let it get to that point, BigHead Wang.

21

HOW TO PULL OFF AN IMPRESSIVE JOB INTERVIEW

All of us are intent on finding the perfect occupation, and only one cruel thing stands in our way: the job interview.

Nothing strikes more fear into the hearts of career-oriented adults than the dreaded job interview. Why? Because it's intrinsically unknown. It's tricky. It's the seed beneath a forest of self-doubt.

If things go too smoothly in a job interview, it's probably because you screwed up. If the experience was rocky, it's probably because you screwed up. If you called the interviewer "Mr. Lambada" when his name was actually Mr. Lentana, then you definitely screwed up. There are thousands of ways to muck up a job interview, from dressing wrongly to having a bad hair day to not knowing enough about the company beforehand.

That encouragement aside, there are also a number of things to keep in mind that can help you get off on the right foot. It's no day at the beach, but it doesn't have to be as hard as you think. Here are a few tips to take the edge off the stress.

SHAKE LIKE A MAN (OR WOMAN)

A firm handshake is always, always appropriate for both male and female job applicants. It projects confidence. It creates a vital first impression. And for many interviewers, it even hints at personality—according to a study by the University of Alabama, people with a strong handshake were found to be, as a rule, more confident than the fish-wristed.[1] The handshake is the first (and usually only) physical contact between you and your interviewer, so it needs to be done right.

SUGGESTIONS:

- Prevent your hands from becoming too sweaty by keeping them open—don't ball them into fists before the handshake. You might also keep a tissue in your pocket to surreptitiously wipe off excessive sweat. Most of all, don't worry too much about sweaty palms. We all have them, and if you think about it too much, you'll probably make it worse. (So, um ... good luck on that one.)
- Make eye contact during the handshake. The strongest handshake can turn sour if you refuse to look at your interviewer.
- Grip in moderation—not too firm, not too weak. As a general rule, assume the grip is going to be strong and match it.

DRESS APPROPRIATELY

According to researchers at the University of Toledo, job applicants have less than thirty seconds to make their mark on

---

1. William F. Chaplin, PhD, Jeffrey B. Phillips, Jonathan D. Brown, Nancy R. Clanton, and Jennifer L. Stein, "Handshaking, Gender, Personality and First Impressions," *Journal of Personality and Social Psychology*, Vol. 79, No. 1.

interviewers.[2] First impressions are vital in the interview process, and—like it or not—most first impressions are gleaned from the way you look. Clothing is critical. You should dress professionally, conservatively, and look as if you'd fit immediately into that workplace. Here's the rule: Find out how the company's best-dressed people clothe themselves, then dress accordingly. Even if you're applying for a company that enjoys casual days, you need to dress up. In most cases, this will mean a suit for men (dark socks and shoes, white shirt, conservative tie). For women, dark suits also look professional, though you have more options (a colorful blouse is fine). Wear jewelry in moderation, plus comfortable heels and hose.

ADDITIONAL TIPS:

- Some employers admit to sneaking a peek at the watch of the person they're interviewing and forming an impression as a result. That means no fluorescent Space Ghost watches with Velcro straps—even if that's what you usually wear.

- Guys, make sure your shirt collar is crisply ironed and clean. Interviewers will spend 90 percent of their time focused on your face and neck. You don't want them staring at a rumpled, dirty collar.

- Ladies, keep your long hair pulled back so people can see your eyes and face. This will also prevent you from twiddling with it when you get nervous.

SHOW CONFIDENCE

You will be advertising both yourself and your abilities. It's a balancing act—you don't want to come across as too meek, nor do you want to annoy your interviewer with arrogance. Don't brag or boast too much, but don't sell yourself short by any means. Smile. Be attentive. Above all, make eye contact. Failure to do so may

2. Jenni Laidman, "Making an Impression," *The Topeka Capital-Journal* (posted June 25, 2001, at *www.cjonline.com/stories/062501/pro_impressions.shtml*).

indicate shyness or even deceit. Neither is ideal for landing a job.

The biggest challenge for many job applicants will be nervousness. Remember that *everyone* is nervous for interviews, and interviewers expect it. But don't let your apprehension get the best of you. Among other things, an interviewer will consider how you might handle the job based on how you handle the interview. If the tension makes your voice crack and your ears sweat, they'll take note.

On the other hand, if you prepare by studying your résumé, mentally outlining goals and objectives, and anticipating potential questions, you're more likely to remain poised. Confidence in yourself will convince the interviewer you can handle the job. Just don't be overbearing or aggressive. An up-front, honest appraisal of your talents and abilities is expected and admired. A know-it-all is not.

KNOW THE COMPANY

If I want to work for XYZ International, it might be a good idea to find out exactly what kind of work XYZ International does. Not only is it common courtesy to know something about the company you're applying to work for, it's also common sense. You don't want to find out after the fact that the product you've been hired to market is illegal in thirty-seven states and an embarrassment to your mother.

Yet surprisingly, failure to research the prospective company is one of the biggest mistakes job applicants make these days. You will most likely be asked this question: "So tell me, what do you know about our company?"

There's no reason not to know that answer. Get online. Look up the company's Web site or Google their name. Poke around. With a little searching, you can weed out the company's products and services, reputation, leadership, and possibly even its recent market performance. Upon answering the above question, don't rattle off so much information that you seem like a weird corporate stalker. Offer just enough to let the interviewer know you've done your research. It'll earn you respect and make you seem smart. That's good.

PRACTICE YOUR ANSWERS

Certain questions—like the aforementioned "what do you know about our company?"—are asked in almost every job interview. Your challenge is to make sure you're prepared for them. Don't count on being able to successfully ad-lib replies to questions like "What is your greatest weakness?" or "What challenging work issue have you recently faced, and how did you handle it?"

Almost any career resource center or interview-prep Web site will have a collection of potential questions to expect. Study them. Have concrete examples ready in response to questions about your most significant personal and professional accomplishments. Be ready to describe both short- and long-term goals. Know your strengths and weaknesses. Above all, practice your answers.

A good idea is to have a friend ask questions, then honestly measure your response. While it may seem corny to do so, it's better to look like a dork to your roommate than to stumble in the interview, rambling about lost loves and mediocre athletic accomplishments after being asked nothing more difficult than "How would you describe yourself?"

ASK THE RIGHT QUESTIONS

At the end of an interview, you'll be given the chance to ask your own questions. *Always* take advantage of this opportunity. Ask a question, if for no other reason than to continue to express interest in the company and position.

What do you ask? Start with the company itself. Ask how it has changed in the past three to five years. Ask how the current economy has altered the day-to-day operations. Ask about the company's goals. Where does it expect to be within five years?

Or ask for any position-related details that haven't yet been covered. What are its main objectives? What kinds of obstacles can you expect? Does the employer see the position's responsibilities changing soon? Should you be hired, what would be your first project or goal?

Asking attentive, knowledgeable questions at the end of the interview serves two purposes. It shows interviewers that you're thoughtful and focused, which helps them decide whether you're right for the job. Secondly, by clarifying the status of the company and details of the position, questions can help you decide whether the job's right for you.

On the other hand, *don't* ask the wrong questions. Don't bring up salary or compensation in the first interview (that's a more appropriate question for follow-up interviews). Don't ask when you'll get your first raise. Don't ask when you'll be promoted. Don't ask about the hours or how soon you can go on vacation or whether there's a decorating budget for your office. In short, don't give them any reason to dislike or distrust you in the first meeting.

FINAL WORDS

At the end of the interview, express your genuine interest in the position. (A perceived lack of enthusiasm for the job can be a red flag for interviewers.) Tell them you want the job. Ask about the next step in the process. Thank him or her for their time, and leave with a positive, confident handshake. After the interview, be sure to send a thank-you note or email.

Remember—people who get jobs aren't necessarily the most accomplished or best-qualified applicants. In many cases, they were the ones who interviewed the best. Like any acting performance, preparation is critical. You have to know your character, your lines, your part. Interviewing by the seat of your pants only works if you're an underwear model.

CHAPTER TWENTY-TWO

ROMANCE DOESN'T ALWAYS HAVE TO BE EXPENSIVE

In any dating, engaged, or married relationship, it's important to maintain the thing that brought the couple together in the first place: romance. Without romance, a marriage can be little more than an economic and social partnership, a mutually beneficial lifestyle choice. It's like using a television set to fill the rectangular void in your entertainment center, but never actually turning it on—everything looks like it belongs, but the object itself is being wasted. It's not living up to its potential.

Or to use another dorky metaphor, romance is the water that causes the seed of a relationship to grow. Problem is, we're all going thirsty because we're intimidated by the watering process. Romance looks too hard. It seems too expensive.

And it's all Hollywood's fault. Seriously. Most of us take our cues on how the world works from the media. Here's a test: In your mind, picture a romantic dinner. Most likely, your vision involves a white linen tablecloth, silver serving platters, and crystal stemware in an intimate, hushed atmosphere. Why? Because the venue for a romantic dinner in movies and television is most often a fancy restaurant. Same goes for romantic gifts (jewelry) and flowers (a dozen red roses). When was the last time a guy showed up for a date on TV with a bouquet of daisies? Or a single *white* rose?

Romance doesn't have to be expensive, and it doesn't have to be about the same clichés you see all the time on television and in the movies. Fancy restaurants and long-stemmed roses are no guarantees of romance. In fact, the most romantic gestures are more likely to be easier on the wallet. Why? Because they are personal. They are creative. They may take time and effort, but they aren't mass-produced. They aren't for sale somewhere, and that's what makes them romantic.

So, near-adult person, consider this: The most romantic activities are often the most economical. Here's why.

BEING ROMANTIC IS ABOUT THE SMALL STUFF

For any romantic relationship to develop and thrive—husband and wife, boyfriend and girlfriend, film geek and Kevin Smith—there must be some sort of intimate connection. Intimacy is wrapped up in details: the way she twirls her hair when she's nervous, the way he shivers when you brush your fingers against the back of his neck. That kind of familiarity requires the interplay of thoughts, hopes, dreams, fears—all wrapped up in tiny, fragile moments of transparency with each other.

So why propose marriage on the Jumbotron at the next Dodgers game?

As relationships expert Greg Godek once put it, romance is "much more about the small gestures—the little ways of making daily life with your lover a bit more special"—than it is about the big, gaudy, extravagant stuff.[1]

The small gestures are the things you do that break from the daily routine and let your loved one know that he or she is special. It's stuff like a stickie-note on the steering wheel that says "I love you" or the phone call in the middle of the day just to say "hi." Other small gestures: holding hands in public; bringing home a favorite flower; making your own bookmark (with a special note) and putting it inside the book she's reading; sitting with him on the couch to watch the game (the *whole* game); walking in the door with an ice cream treat; arranging to have a note, a flower, or breakfast left on his desk at work; telling her you love her at unexpected or inappropriate times (like during the movie or at the top of the roller coaster or during a sermon).

BEING ROMANTIC IS ABOUT THE UNEXPECTED

One of the major evils of the developed world is the Romantic Mandate. There are a handful of days on our calendar—like Valentine's Day, Christmas, or a birthday—at which time those in romantic relationships must meet the societal directive of romanticism. You'd *better* get your loved one a gift and a card on those days, because if you don't, you're toast. For that reason, Valentine's gifts are usually uninspired boxes of chocolates or bouquets of roses. The card is something you grabbed at Wal-Mart on the way home, body-checking your way through the throng of sweaty, nervous men swarming the American Greetings aisle. The result is hardly special and no different from what every other male in the world is doing. Godek calls these "obligatory romance days," events you are required to remember and act upon, but for which you get exactly zero props.[2] None. Roses on February 14? Unoriginal, unimaginative, and downright expensive. Sorry. Doesn't count. Not romantic.

What's truly romantic is a gift that comes out of nowhere, like a bouquet of roses a week *before* Valentine's Day. Or a rose a day for the twelve days leading up to it.[3] Or instead of a fancy Valentine's dinner out (just like everyone else is doing), rent her favorite DVD and garnish it with pizza and a bottle of bubbly. Or simply offer a foot rub without being asked.

You see where we're going with this? Whether it's for Valentine's Day or Columbus Day, a gift is romantic not because of the price, but because of the sentiment—the thought and effort put into it. A well-timed greeting card given on an otherwise uneventful day will be treasured more than an expensive birthday gift for one simple reason: the card is neither compulsory nor expected. No one made you do it.

BEING ROMANTIC IS ABOUT CREATIVITY

A romantic gesture is cherished when the experience of it is completely unique. It's when the recipient knows he or she is the only person opening this gift, reading this card, or enjoying this moment. How do you do it? Refuse to settle for the status quo.

Are you the kind of person who buys a nice greeting card, signs your name inside, and stuffs it into the envelope? If so, you are a pox on the male species. The rules of creative romance dictate that you make greeting cards personal. This means writing a personal note in every card you give—even if it's as simple as "I love you because ..." and then listing one or two good qualities. Simply putting your name on something Hallmark designed and wrote requires no

2. Godek, p. 41.
3. Here's a secret: Twelve single, unadorned roses bought separately will end up being less expensive than a dozen roses elaborately arranged into a bouquet. Score one for both creativity and frugality.

thought or effort whatsoever. You might as well find a card that says, "I'm too lazy for anything else," and then sign your name to it. Mass production = Bad.

Of course, not everyone's a writer, and many are uncomfortable putting thoughts into coherent words. Here's a solution: Get creative with quantity instead of quality. One guy bought his wife a box of Scooby-Doo kids' valentines, the small ones children give their teachers and friends. He wrote simple little notes in all thirty (i.e. "You're pretty" or "I love you") and left them around the house, in her car, in her purse—all over the place—for her to find throughout the day. Big winner. The gift was much less expensive than a box of chocolates and far more memorable.

A bouquet of flowers is generally not too creative—but a bouquet of something *other* than flowers is. For instance, multiples of her favorite candy or a basket of bathtub stuff (soaps, oils, lotions). And who says guys don't like a bouquet? Most guys would be perfectly happy to accept, for instance, a collection of socket wrenches. Or movie tickets. Or gift cards to their favorite restaurants. Find ways to fit the gift to the recipient, and you're on your way to romance.

FINAL WORDS

Relationships are hard enough without being complicated by the money issue. In a world where going out is activity-oriented, it's hard to date when you're poor. It's harder still to be married on a budget. But simple, thoughtful romance greases the relationship wheel, and though romance *can* cost a fortune, it certainly doesn't have to. What it does cost, without fail, is a little time and effort. It means going out of your way to bring happiness to the one you love. And if you can't bring yourself to do that, then maybe you should first ask yourself this: Am I really in love?

23

BUY GROCERIES LIKE YOU OWN THE SUPERMARKET

Grocery shopping is serious business. Money is involved. Personal opinion comes into play. Detailed knowledge is required. People judge you based on the cereal in your shopping cart. Others count the items in your basket to make sure you're not committing an express-lane infraction. No, a trip to the grocery store is not to be taken lightly. How to do it right is one of the things every grownup needs to know.

THE BASICS

Here are a few grocery-shopping rules to get started, all meticulously researched and field-tested in order to make your supermarket experience a success. Or whatever.

Know what you need before you go. If you shop once a week, plan your week's menu prior to the trip. Check the pantry to see if anything's running low. You don't want to buy something you already have, nor do you want to come home only to find out you're low on flour. Make a list.

Calculate how much you'll need. Buying in bulk saves money, unless half the product goes to waste or gets thrown away once you've grown tired of it. Don't buy jumbo-sized boxes of Chocolate Frosted Sugar Bombs if you won't finish them off. Large quantities are only economical once they're gone.

Eat before you shop. Supermarkets smell, look, and feel good. The produce glistens, the bread is piping hot, and the aroma in the coffee aisle alone is enough to give you the shakes. If you enter this environment on an empty stomach, you'll fall prey to impulse buys and a grocery bill that expands as fast as your waistline. Eat first and you'll have a much easier time sticking to your list.

Be adventurous. Did you know that grocery stores' most profitable (read: expensive) products are usually at eye level? That's because marketing research indicates you're more likely to buy the first product you see. The best values require bending and stretching, and most often are the "house" brands—the less-expensive, non-national products. Fact is, they're pretty much the same as the big brands (consistent nutritional quality is required by the FDA) but without the expensive packaging and marketing costs. Generics have come a long way from the black-and-white label stigma of your childhood. Don't be a corporate tool. Take a chance on a generic.

Be aware. The eye-level thing isn't the only trick grocery stores have behind their aprons. There's a reason you have to walk all the way to the back of the store—past aisle upon aisle of cookies and cereal—just to grab a gallon of milk. And those end-of-the-aisle displays that make it look like a product is on sale?

Sometimes there's no sale at all. But we're suckers for the feeling of accomplishment we get when we think we've discovered a good deal, and we'll buy something we don't need just to pat ourselves on the back. So we end up with two bags of chips and an armful of soft drinks that weren't on our list.

Talk to the employees. They can tell you when fruit, vegetable, and dairy shipments arrive, whether it's daily or hourly. Becoming aware of their schedule allows you to plan accordingly and come home with fresher, longer-lasting groceries.

Scan the scanner. Even in today's heavily wired supermarkets, mistakes can be made in the checkout process, particularly when it comes to sale items. Keep your eyes on the display. It's better to catch an error as it occurs than to come back and quibble over a twenty-cent difference in the price of your sliced olives. If there's one thing you don't want to be known for, it's being all weird about your olives.

THE SPECIFICS: FRUITS

It's easy to buy a can of sliced peaches or mandarin oranges because someone else does the choosing for you. But everyone knows the best value and nutrition can be found in fresh produce, so top shoppers avoid canned foods. Here are some specific things to know.

APPLES. Look for a deep, uniform color with few blemishes, soft spots, or indentions.

BANANAS. Look for a firm, uniform color and don't be afraid to buy them a little green—they're much sweeter when tinged with green, and they'll ripen at home. Avoid the soft or spotted ones.

BERRIES. Except for blueberries, most berries are very perishable. Strawberries should be red, firm, and plump, like a clown's nose. When buying blackberries, raspberries, or boysenberries, look for firm, solid, plump product. Avoid berries that are starting to soften or "juice" or look moldy. You'll need to use them pretty soon after they've been washed.

CANTALOUPE. To check for ripeness, gently press the large indentation on the end of the melon. It should give slightly. Then give it a sniff: A ripe melon will have a sweet, fragrant aroma.

GRAPES. Look for bunches that are firm and clustered tightly to the stems. Seedless are best. Store grapes uncovered in your fridge for optimum crispness.

LEMONS AND LIMES. Should feel heavy for their size and have a deep yellow (lemon) or dark green (lime) color. Avoid thick-skinned lemons and soft, wrinkly limes.

ORANGES. The heavier the better. You want smooth, thin skins without withered or discolored areas.[1]

PEACHES. Should be firm and uniform in color, with a rosy blush. Ripe ones will smell sweet and give under slight pressure.

WATERMELON. Two fun ways to check for ripeness. First, scrape the outer rind with your fingernail; you should get a thin green shaving. Second, give it a thump. A ripe watermelon will respond with a hollow thud.

ONE MORE TIP: Because fruits are perishable, they require lots of attention in the store and need to be handled carefully. That means every time you squeeze, poke, or shake them, you're possibly damaging the fruit for yourself or the next shopper. So as you check for ripeness, be considerate: Less pestering equals longer life.

THE SPECIFICS: VEGGIES

Vegetables are good for you. They are chock-full of nutrients, naturally low in fat, and will fill you up with fiber. Like fruits, fresh vegetables can be identified by their bright, bold colors. They need to be handled carefully to keep bruising to a minimum and can be

1. You can tell whether the skin is thick or thin by squeezing the fruit slightly. A thinner peel will be much more flexible.

safely stored in your fridge for two to five days. Don't buy more than you can use in that amount of time.

ASPARAGUS. You want closed, compact tips in a rich green color. Avoid tips that are open, too wide, or too long.

BROCCOLI. Look for the ones with tight dark green (even purplish) buds.

CARROTS. The best ones are smaller: less than six inches in length, an inch in diameter at the widest point, and bright orange. Avoid the really big ones, the soft or flabby ones, and the ones that look "woody."[2]

CORN. Look for a blunt ear, dark and dry silk, and kernels that spurt juice when you slice them with a fingernail (not that anyone told you to go around doing that).

LETTUCE. Each variety can be different, but generally you want a crisp, non-wilted texture, and a good bright color. Most may have some sort of discoloration on the outer leaves, which is normal, but you should watch out for major decay. Iceberg is the most popular lettuce, but Romaine offers more nutrients and, some say, better taste.

ONIONS. The best onions are firm, dry, and slightly flat. They should have dry necks and be reasonably free from blemishes. By the way, onions release eye-irritating sulfur compounds when you cut them—that's why they cause tears. The only way to avoid this is to cut them in running water. Or to stay away from onions.

POTATOES. Potatoes store fairly well, so they can be purchased in bulk. Avoid rot, a greenish tint, sprouts, or sunken eyes.

TOMATOES.[3] The heavier, the better. Ripe tomatoes will be a deep solid red and yield to pressure. If necessary, they can ripen during storage. Try grape or cherry tomatoes as a snack—they're bite-sized and sweeter than the big ones.

---

2. Okay, just stop right there, gutter-brain. We know what you're thinking.
3. Yes, tomatoes are technically a fruit. But no one ever thinks of them that way, so for our purposes here, they're veggies.

THE SPECIFICS: BEEF AND POULTRY

Now, on to the main course. According to the U.S. Department of Agriculture (USDA), there are three primary grades of beef. USDA Prime is the top-tier stuff because it has the most marbling (the small white specks of fat which make the beef juicier and more flavorful without adding a lot of cholesterol). Most USDA Prime beef is sold to restaurants—rarely will you find it at a grocery store or even a butcher shop. Only 2 percent of all beef is worthy of this distinction. This is what cows aspire to.

Supermarket beef will usually be graded at the next two levels: USDA Choice and USDA Select. Choice has pretty good marbling (though considerably less than prime) and makes a great steak. USDA Select has the least marbling of the three. It also has fewer calories but will not be as tender, juicy, or flavorful. Because it's cheaper to buy on the wholesale level, Select is usually what you'll find at the big supercenters or discount stores.

HERE'S WHAT TO LOOK FOR, BESIDES THE LABEL:

Beef should be a bright red with white flecks of marbling. It should have no gray spots. If the beef has been vacuum-packed, it probably won't turn red until a few minutes after the package is opened—that color is the result of interaction with oxygen.

Firm is good, mushy is not. Discoloration is not. Lots of extra fat is not. Offensive odors are, obviously, not. And, yes, we're still talking about beef, not what to look for in a potential date.

Check the tray for excess liquid—you don't want it. Because 99 percent of the blood is drained from the carcass at the slaughterhouse, any liquid you see is probably excess moisture that has leaked out.[4] The presence of moisture may indicate the beef has recently been stored at too high of a temperature, allowing bacteria

---

4. It's probably best not to bring up these kinds of factoids during basic dinner table conversation, nor to use words like "carcass" or "slaughterhouse" in any discussion about meat. People are sensitive. Just FYI.

to grow and the taste to decline.

Check the packaging, too. You don't want torn or punctured plastic wrap. And make sure you're buying before the "sell by" date on the label.

Beef keeps in your freezer for six to twelve months; ground beef for three months. Wrap it in foil or an airtight plastic bag—*not* on the plastic tray it comes in—and when you're ready to eat it, thaw it in the fridge to prevent the growth of harmful bacteria (see chapter 6).

As for chicken, the easiest way to buy it is in individual cuts— i.e. boneless breasts or individual drumsticks. This can be more expensive than buying an entire chicken, but who wants to do all the separating themselves? Not me. Not you either.

A chicken breast should have smooth and tender skin, with well-distributed fat and no blemishes. As usual, avoid torn or damaged packaging. When storing, keep the chicken refrigerated. To freeze it, remove it from the original packaging and place it in airtight, moisture-proof plastic. Thaw in the fridge or microwave—not at room temperature, which you should know by now.

FINAL WORDS

Unless you live under an oppressive totalitarian regime, grocery shopping is rarely a life-and-death matter. It is, however, an activity that requires a combination of purchasing skill and experience behind the shopping cart. Getting the best value and the freshest produce involves a little time and effort, but it's necessary for those consumers whose culinary tastes have progressed beyond peanut-butter-and-jelly.

And, believe me, that's who you want to be.

CHAPTER TWENTY-FOUR

PAW-PAW AND THE VALUE OF STORIES

When I was a kid, I thought I knew my grandfather, John Boyett. Paw-Paw had a broad nose and a neck crisscrossed with wrinkles. He smelled like a blend of the minty Copenhagen he dipped and the sawdust of his workshop. He built stuff, and he had all kinds of tools. He watched *The Today Show* during breakfast and listened to Paul Harvey at lunch. He sang a barrel-deep bass.

I thought I knew Paw-Paw, until, around the age of twelve, I attended an air show with him. One of the aircraft on display was an old, World War II–era B-17 Bomber, the legendary "flying fortress." Paw-Paw took me aboard. As we climbed inside, he began to tell me about the plane: where the bombs were stored and how they were released, where the guns were stationed and the size of the bullets, what kinds of missions the planes flew and in what theaters.

"How do you know so much about this airplane?" I asked from the back of the fuselage.

"Because I was sitting right about where you are when we got shot down." My eyes grew as wide as Paw-Paw's nose, but he kept talking.

"The wings caught fire, and the heat was about to weld the door shut. I couldn't see anything because of the smoke. So I backed up right there"—he pointed to the fuselage wall opposite the hatch through which we'd just entered—"and I jumped at the door with both feet. Went right through and started falling until I remembered to open my parachute." Then his voice dropped an octave. "Most of my buddies died."

Based in Italy, my grandfather was on one of his last bombing runs as a twenty-one-year-old side-gunner and flight engineer when his plane encountered enemy fire over Austria. After reluctantly bailing from his post—and his plane—he parachuted directly into Nazi territory. Paw-Paw ended up in a succession of German prisoner-of-war camps. He spent more than a year in captivity, subsisting on watery "stew" and thinking he'd never see his family again. He held on mentally by reading and rereading a bundle of letters from his bride, Mary Ellen, whom he'd left behind in Hollis, Oklahoma.

His escape came as suddenly as his capture. Paw-Paw and a number of other prisoners were eventually herded out of the camp and forced into a cross-country trek at the end of winter, in temperatures so cold he had to set fire to his precious letters to keep his fingers from freezing. "It was intended to be our death march," he says now. After two weeks, the captors and prisoners neared the Germany-Poland border. Without warning, a Jeep crested the hill ahead of them, driven by a British colonel who'd become lost and accidentally veered into enemy territory. Paw-Paw's German guards assumed it was the lead vehicle in an Allied onslaught, and they fled. The prisoners stood there stunned, alone, and shivering. They had stumbled into freedom, liberated by a Brit's bad navigation.

I thought I knew Paw-Paw until I heard him tell this story inside the hollow shell of a vintage airplane. His version is usually punctuated with much greater detail, buttressed by self-deprecating humor, and, occasionally, some sadness. He tells it rarely. It's a powerful story, but a difficult one—he didn't speak of those events at all until many years after the war. I realize now there is much I don't know about my grandfather. The man I *do* know was made during those months as a POW, during that march, upon that liberation. To know Paw-Paw is to know his story.

Next time you're at an office party or backyard barbecue, look around. Who has an audience? Who commands the group's attention? Here's a hint: It's not the guy near the grill trying to impress with collections of facts. It's not the blowhard pushing a political agenda. Nope. It's the storyteller, the one who reveals himself, his history, his experiences to the group by way of adventure. He entertains us, and we feel most comfortable in *his* presence—because in knowing part of his story, we feel we know a part of him.

Stories are the lifeblood of our culture. Good employees, good friends, good leaders—all have learned to appreciate one another's stories. Here's what they know.

STORIES HELP US RELATE

A 1998 article in *The New York Times* detailed an Internet study by Carnegie-Mellon University. Researchers hooked up 169 individuals in Pittsburgh with free computers and Internet service beginning in 1995. The participants answered a series of questions at the start of the study, then again a couple of years later. The questions measured social contacts, depression, stress, and loneliness. You can guess the punchline. In this, the first real study of the social and psychological effects of home Internet usage, the researchers found that people who spend even a handful of hours online have higher levels of loneliness than those who use the computer less frequently. According to the article, the research raised "troubling questions about the nature of virtual communication and the disembodied relationships found in cyberspace."[1]

Via the Internet, those study participants undoubtedly came into contact with more people than they had previously—that's one of the benefits of online communities. But how deep was that contact? Was it trite message board chatter? Hastily scrawled emails? Useless variations on "Hi. How R U?"

Aside from a few powerful blog and message board communities, there's a social element missing from most online activity: the power of stories to build and sustain relationships. The problem today is that we've conceded the reins of storytelling over to the media. The plush cineplex and the ever-widening television screen have replaced the dinner table as the primary forum for stories. That's fine on one hand; some are better storytellers than others, and their voices should be heard. What's not so good is that the human element is missing. You can't really interact with a movie (unless, of course, it's *The Rocky Horror Picture Show*).

STORIES HELP US RESPECT

I used to produce marketing materials for a local retirement community. Over the course of that job, I wrote editorial profiles of

1. Amy Harmon, "Sad, Lonely World Discovered in Cyberspace," *New York Times* (August 30, 1998) p. A3. Though the results of this study are telling, the research itself is probably flawed. A sample of 169 is hardly broad enough to merit the melodramatic title given it by the newspaper. And no indication is made as to whether the participants were already depressed and lonely to begin with. After all, Pittsburgh *can* be dreary.

that community's active residents and volunteers, men and women whose past experiences never ceased to surprise me. There's nothing more fun than the transformation of a demure grandmother into a storytelling force when asked about her childhood. I met frail widows who flew for the Civilian Air Force. I spoke with stooped men who had shaken the hands of presidents. I profiled inventors, business pioneers, and authors, including a kind, petite, eighty-year-old woman who wrote dozens of pulp Westerns during the '60s and '70s under a masculine pseudonym. When I first met these individuals, they were little more than names, room numbers, nursing home residents, or retirees. When the interviews were over, they had become inspirations.

It's easy to feel uncomfortable around people who are different from us—the elderly, the sick, the foreign. At the same time, that discomfort is largely based on the unfamiliar. Whether we admit it or not, we shy away from the unknown. We see a face, a skin color, a collection of wrinkles, and we construct a one-dimensional character sketch—Bitter, Dangerous, Senile—to inject information into the void.

But we can't stop there. When we ask questions and listen to the answers, that discomfort begins to decrease, and the unknown becomes known. Stories humanize us. They break through our prejudices. When we know someone's story, we've encountered what's real and discarded the flimsy caricature. That's respect.

STORIES HELP US REMEMBER

It is said that each generation shares at least one common story—one that, in some way or another, serves to define and unite that generation. For our grandparents, that story is the attack on Pearl Harbor and the war years that followed. For our parents, it was the

Kennedy assassination. For us, of course, our common story was written in September of 2001. At work that morning, watching the one television set in my building along with my coworkers, I had the strangest thought: "Remember this. This is where you were when it happened." I memorized the faces in the room with me, the slant of sunlight through the windows, the dust on the TV screen.

Why? Because I knew it would be a chapter in my story, and an important one. Most of what I now know about my grandfather wasn't revealed to me that day at the air show, but a few years later on a Saturday afternoon. It was during my junior year of high school, and I was finishing an assignment for my U.S. History class. The assignment was to ask someone where they were and how they felt upon hearing about Pearl Harbor and to record their answer. I asked Paw-Paw. His answer: "I was in Hollis, on the farm, and I was angry. I enlisted the next morning." That statement was followed by two hours of revelation about the war. I met Paw-Paw that afternoon.

Someday, our kids or grandkids will ask us about September 11th. When they do, they'll meet something new in us.

FINAL WORDS

Stories are societal glue. Since the earliest tribes first squatted around a fire, stories have been our connection to one another. They help us understand. They illustrate who we are. They shape who we will become. What's your story?

25

SIMPLE HOME MAINTENANCE WHEN DAD'S UNAVAILABLE

Best realization upon moving into your own place: "Hey. I'm still in my underwear, and nobody cares!"

Worst realization upon moving into your own place: "The toilet's doing what? Where's Dad?"

Most fathers are good at a number of things, and one of those usually involves taking care of stuff around the house. Dispensing advice is another, so most of us have heard something along the lines of this statement: Take care of your home, because it sure can't take care of itself.

Houses age. They deteriorate. And because they're your largest and most valuable asset, the last thing you want is for your home to fall into disrepair. That's why simple home maintenance is essential. It protects your financial investment and property value. It provides a safe, healthy environment for you and your family. And it minimizes repair work and expense—it's a whole lot easier to work to prevent the development of unsafe conditions and structural damage than to foot the bill once things fall apart.

Your monthly budget should include some money set aside for taking care of your home. Experts suggest putting back 1 to 3 percent of your home's value each year for regular upkeep. Every six months you should visually inspect your house and yard to identify trouble spots. Then, make the trouble spots go away. You can always hire professionals to do some tasks, but many precautionary ones are simple enough to do on your own. And much, much cheaper.

Following are some of those regular home maintenance tasks. This is the kind of stuff Dad used to do. If you're under a roof of your own now, male or female, this stuff is now *your* job.

MONTHLY MAINTENANCE

1. Check the pressure gauge on your fire extinguisher(s), which should be kept near your kitchen stove and any wood-burning fireplace.

2. Test smoke detectors and replace batteries if necessary.

3. Check your heating and/or cooling air filters. Clean or replace them if necessary. Some filters need to be changed monthly; others are good for three months or more, depending on the type and quality. Check your owner's manual for recommendations.

4. Clear gutters and downspouts of debris (leaves, dirt, action figures). Check for loose connections, rust, signs of leakage. Make sure they are properly secured and that there is no blockage in the discharge area.

5. Examine shower and/or bathtub enclosures. Replace deteriorated grout and caulk if necessary. Caulk that has become cracked or brittle is useless as a water seal. Remove it and bead

on a long-lasting material like silicone or latex. While you're at it, look for signs of leakage beneath plumbing fixtures. Remove hair from drains (everyone now: *yeeesh*) and make sure it drains properly. If not, try a liquid cleaner, an auger (also known as a snake), or a plunger.

6. Check all plumbing connections beneath sinks and toilets. Look for leaks at shut-off valves for sinks, toilets, your washer and dryer, and the main water shut-off valve. If necessary, replace leaky faucets or shower heads.

7. Make sure your toilet flushes correctly, doesn't run continuously (usually the result of a defective seal), and is properly secured to the floor. Believe me, no one likes a loose potty. Wait ... that may need to be reworded.

8. Check ground-fault circuit interrupter devices (GFCIs) in your bathrooms, kitchen, and garage by pressing the test button.

SEASONAL MAINTENANCE (SPRING AND FALL)

1. Get up on the roof and look for damage (especially if you live in a hail-prone area). Check for wounded shingles, tiles, or other roof coverings, including chimney and flashing. **HINT**: "Roof flashing" may sound a little perv and possibly criminal, but don't worry—it's just the name for the sheet metal used to reinforce and weatherproof your roof's joints and angles.

2. Climb into the attic, if possible, and make sure your roof vents are unobstructed by insulation or anything else. If light from the outside shines through, you're probably okay. Check for vermin activity. (According to popular cartoons, mice often collect spools of thread, thimbles, and empty sardine tins for furniture, so be on the lookout for artful, domestic arrangements of such.) Level out the insulation to cover bare spots, if necessary, and make sure no loose wiring is exposed.

3. Give your home exterior a once-over. Trim back tree branches and shrubs so they don't scrape against the house. Look for loose mortar joints around bricks. Check siding for loose or missing pieces, and check for cracking and separating on stucco walls. Watch for loose or decaying trim. Make sure all caulking that joins two different materials (such as where window trim meets siding) is in good condition. Do you see peeling, cracked, or mildewed paint? Birds' nests? Rival gang graffiti?

4. Examine basement or crawl space walls for evidence of moisture seepage. Make sure all landscaping encourages water to flow away from your foundation.

5. Inspect porch, deck, driveway, and all sidewalks for deterioration, movement, or anything else that can pose a safety hazard. For instance, rattlesnakes.

6. Make sure your windows close, lock, and seal properly. Inspect them for loose putty, holes in screens, and evidence of moisture between pane and storm windows. Look for cracked or broken glass.

7. Check the inside and outside of all foundation walls for termite activity. It may be a good idea to get an extermination service to do this for you. They know what to look for.

8. Test your overhead garage door opener to make sure the auto-reverse mechanism works. To do so, let it close on a two-by-four, a brick, or a bucket. The door should stop and reverse quickly upon touching the object. If it stops but doesn't reverse, decrease the down-force a quarter-turn or so. Repeat the test until the door reverses. You may also want to clean and lubricate hinges, rollers, and tracks.

ANNUAL MAINTENANCE

1. Have your chimney(s) cleaned and inspected each winter before you begin using it regularly. Buildup of soot and creosote can keep it

from drafting properly and can potentially cause a chimney fire.

2. Look for water damage, exposed wires, or any signs of wear in your electrical service panels. If you have a fuse that blows often or a circuit breaker that trips frequently, call an electrician to figure out the problem and repair it. Make sure each circuit is clearly marked so you know which outlets or appliances are connected to it.

3. Check the temperature-pressure relief valve on the water heater, which guards against hazardous pressure buildup. Lift up or depress the handle (water should drain from the overflow pipe). Check for leaking or rusting. Some manufacturers recommend that a small amount of water be drained periodically from the tank to reduce sediment buildup. Let it flow into a bucket until the water looks clear.

4. Clean and inspect all systems and service appliances as suggested by the manufacturer's recommendations. Some warranties—especially on heating and cooling systems—may be voided if you fail to have an authorized serviceperson inspect them once a year (or as stated otherwise).

5. Monitor any wall and ceiling surface cracks for evidence of significant movement. Some minor movement should be anticipated due to normal settling and shrinkage. Large gaps, however, are *not* normal.

FINAL WORDS

A lot of this stuff is simple enough to do yourself, but many of us are uncomfortable with anything involving handiness. And that's fine. It's okay to hire a home repair contractor or handyman to oversee some of the above tips. Most of us would be happy to pay a little extra for someone to check the valve behind our toilet if the alternative is, for example, two inches of water on our bathroom floor. Don't be afraid to call in the specialists if you're not comfortable with the task.

Preventive maintenance is the key to keeping your house in good shape. It reduces the risk of unexpected repairs while quietly raising your home's resale value. In fact, if you plan to sell someday, it's a good idea to keep a log or journal of all repairs and improvements during your time in the house. By documenting your upkeep regime, you let future owners know the house has been taken care of, which can make it significantly more attractive.

After all, nothing beats a steady system of personal home inspection and repair. Not even walking around in your underwear.

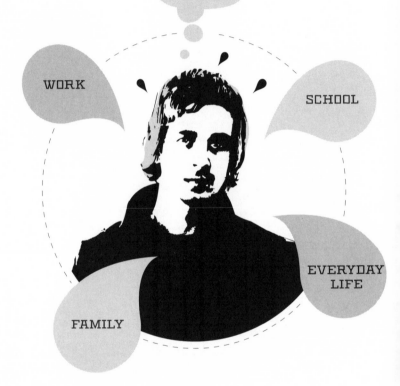

26

DON'T GO TO PIECES: TAKING CARE OF YOUR OWN BAD SELF

From school assignments or on-the-job projects to family responsibilities and, well, everyday life, it's easy to lose perspective. It's easy to put our own physical, mental, and emotional well-being last on our list of priorities. Things can get out of balance—and out of control—pretty quickly.

Sometimes, we really do have to focus on our own needs. To watch out for Number One. It's something every adult needs to know: None of us will get very far if we don't take care of ourselves. Here are the rules for optimum personal performance.

SLEEP LIKE YOU MEAN IT

The best way to run yourself into the ground is to let sleep slip down your priority list. Chronic sleep deprivation—even among young, fit twentysomethings—is associated with a number of health problems, including anxiety and depression. It can stress your cardiovascular system, weaken your immune system, and throw off your hormone levels. It'll also trash your concentration and work performance. Poor sleeping habits have even been linked to heart disease.

So, long story short, it's okay to sleep in a little on Saturdays. In fact, it's probably a good idea. Helpful hints to ensure you're getting enough sleep:

Wind down before you lie down. High-quality sleep usually follows a period of relaxation, so downshift before going to bed. If you exercise at night, do it early enough for your body to cool down before hitting the sack. Take a hot shower or warm bath. Watch *Conan*. Read a book.

Cut the caffeine/nix the nicotine. Nondecaf coffee and smokes, both stimulants, are to sleep what live monkeys are to a liturgical church service. Which is to say, major disruptions. Even if you don't have trouble falling asleep, the quality of your sleep will suffer if you sip or puff before bed—you'll wake up more often, and you'll take longer to reach the deepest, most restful stage of sleep.

Avoid alcohol and heavy meals. While a full stomach and a nightcap might make you drowsy, each can actually keep you from proper rest. Heartburn and indigestion can result in frequent awakenings. Same goes for alcohol. While this doesn't mean you should go to bed on an empty stomach (hunger can keep you up as well), it's wise to schedule the eating and drinking for earlier in the day.

Stick to a schedule. Our bodies are built to follow patterns, and sleeping is no exception. By going to sleep and waking up at approximately the same times every day, your body eases into a healthy sleep pattern. Staying up till dawn or sleeping extravagantly late on weekends—especially if you do it for two days straight—is like jamming a broomstick into bicycle spokes. Problems ensue. Stuff breaks. And Monday won't be very fun.

Check the medical. Some sleep disorders can't be blamed on a late dinner—they could be the result of a medical problem. Physical conditions like sleep apnea, asthma, and congestive heart failure can inhibit proper sleep. So can common infections or viruses and even some over-the-counter medications. If you suspect you might have a problem bigger than a latte nightcap, talk to your doctor or a sleep specialist.

EAT GOOD STUFF

Yes, it's very handy to have a Taco Bell within a mile of your home, particularly when you get a burrito craving at 11:00 p.m. (Now, come on—what did we *just* say about late-night eating?) But, really, the cliché-makers weren't kidding around when they said, "You are what you eat." If you're loading up on fat and grease, don't be surprised when you start to feel fat and greasy.

You're a grownup. You probably know how to eat right, even if you slip up now and then. So let's not spend too much time on this.

JUST A FEW REMINDERS:

Eat a variety of nutritious foods. Scientists say we need more than forty different nutrients to maintain good health, but no one food contains all of them. Not even chocolate. The USDA released an updated version of the trusty food pyramid in May of 2005, and it's still a decent guide to proper eating. Try to get daily servings of fruits and veggies, bread and whole-grain products, milk and dairy, and some kind of protein (meat, poultry, fish, or—for the vegans among us—protein-rich foods like beans or tofu).[1]

Pay special attention to fruits, vegetables, and whole grains. Chances are, rabbits don't even eat enough of this stuff, so how well can *we* measure up? Switch out your plain white sandwich bread for whole-grain wheat. Make a smoothie (check out chapter 13 for more on this). Toss a salad. The best way to make sure you eat enough healthy foods is to keep them handy. When you get the munchies, you're not going to reach for an apple if all you have are Oreos.

Go easy on the portions. Guess what? Experts say the typical restaurant serving is twice as much as you need. Ladies and gentlemen, meet your new best friend: the doggie bag. Use it. Don't clean your plate at one sitting and don't eat until you're uncomfortable ("I'm stuffed. I couldn't eat another bite if I—*hey, cheesecake!*"). Instead, eat half and save the rest for tomorrow. This gives you two meals for the price of one and something to look forward to for lunch the next day.

Don't deprive yourself. What makes extreme diet changes difficult for most of us is that we eat for pleasure. Food isn't just fuel—it tastes *good*. Eating healthy doesn't have to mean giving up everything that contains sugar, fat, or cholesterol. It just means limiting your intake. Hot fudge sundaes are fine, but you don't need one after every meal. Bacon? Enjoy, but stop after a couple of slices. Eat what you love, but keep the portions small and the diet balanced.

MANAGE YOUR TIME WISELY

One of the biggest goofs we make on a daily basis is overburdening ourselves with too many commitments. We have

1. Check out the revamped pyramid at *www.mypyramid.gov.*

too much to do and too little time to do it. Something's gotta give, and if you're not careful, it'll be you. Since we all have the same number of hours a day—and since doing away with sleep isn't an option—then the solution to our time crunch must be to learn how to manage what few minutes we have. By learning to work, live, and play more efficiently, we can discover a whole lot more time than we thought possible.

The best minutes of your day are the ones spent planning and organizing. As a wise man once said—okay, as a poster behind my twelfth grade economics teacher's desk once said—"If you fail to take time for planning, you are planning to fail." Whether it's a simple to-do list or a bells-and-whistles computer app, find what works best for you and stick to it.

Don't procrastinate. Instead of putting big or difficult tasks off, break them down into smaller, bite-sized pieces. At least you'll be doing something.

Combine tasks. Doing two things at once means double productivity, as long as those two things are compatible. (And as long as those two things are not driving to work while sending email on your BlackBerry.) Make to-do lists while you're waiting on hold. Get dressed while you're watching the morning news. Swing by the gas station on your way to the grocery store.

Neglect the trivial. What's more important: Visiting a friend in the hospital or dusting your PEZ collection? Getting your car's oil changed or watching the last ten minutes of *The A-Team*? (Trust me, the plan comes together.) By eliminating or postponing the tasks that aren't as necessary or that don't have long-term consequences, you clear up time for the things that matter.

Be flexible. Management experts often suggest planning for only 50 percent of your time, because the rest will doubtless be lost to temporary distractions or unscheduled urgencies. Expect to be interrupted, but be prepared to get back on track soon after.

Learn to say "no." It's hard to turn down friends and family—but it's also hard to get back on track after your schedule is derailed by something unexpected and, in many cases, not really necessary. "No" is such a small word, but it carries a big stick. Using it regularly frees up time for the things that are most important. Don't be selfish, but don't overburden yourself either.

Enjoy your successes. The joy of keeping a to-do list is found in the much-anticipated "item cross-out." Enjoy it. When you finish a major project, take a moment to relax and strike it from your list. Celebrating the accomplishment nudges you closer to a balanced life. And isn't that the goal of time management?

FINAL WORDS

To review, the best ways to take care of yourself are to sleep well, eat well, and manage your time well. The pressures of life, though intense, can help us become stronger and more confident. But when we start to become overwhelmed, our only defense against those pressures is a commitment to the little things that keep us sane. Carving out opportunities to rest, to stay healthy, to manage our lives—these need to be priorities. So go eat an apple.

CHAPTER TWENTY-SEVEN

ASK FOR A RAISE WITHOUT COMING ACROSS AS A JERK

You got out of college and found a great job. It fits your personality, you like the people there, and—glory of glories—it's actually related to your college major. You're good at it, too. You've played a key role in a couple of recent major successes. Your boss thinks you're a fine employee, the commute is decent, even the coffee is good.

Everything's cool, except for one thing. It's been way too long since you moved up the pay scale. Until now, you've shown the patience of Job, hoping the higher-ups would recognize you for what you bring to the table. But nothing so far. It's time to take matters into your own hands.

It's time to ask for a raise. Here's how to do it.

BE A GOOD EMPLOYEE

To get the golden egg, you first have to build the nest. You have to give your boss a solid reason not to completely laugh in your face when you ask for more. Best way to do it? Be someone he or she can't afford to lose.

Work hard. Be dependable, responsible, and self-sufficient—the kind of employee who doesn't have to be managed. Strive to be both productive and efficient. Show a willingness to come in early, work through lunch, or put in a little overtime as needed. ("As needed" is the key here. If there's one thing managers can't abide, it's clock-milkers.)

Take on more responsibilities. Don't expect your boss to just start forking over more money because you're doing exactly what you were hired to do. Increase your worth by taking on a larger role. Volunteer for big projects. Do more than you're asked. Assuming more responsibilities before asking for a raise gives you better leverage.

Make yourself indispensable. This is related to the first two. If you've developed a reputation for hard work and a willingness to move beyond your job description, then you're the kind of employee a boss can really love. Especially if, along the way, you've been trained for specific tasks or have learned a great deal about the business. Ask this question of yourself: If you weren't around, how hard would it be to replace you? It's much less disruptive to keep a current employee at a higher pay rate than to find, hire, and train someone new to fill your position. The more valuable you are, the further your boss will go to keep you around.

Maintain a good attitude. Let's face it: If you're thinking about asking for a raise, you're not entirely happy with your job, right? Don't let this frustration show. Smile a lot. Listen. Be polite. If you must complain, do it quietly. Above all, be likable. Don't give your boss any reason to deny your request.

DO YOUR RESEARCH

This is your ammunition. When you ask for a raise, you'll need to be prepared to show exactly why you deserve one, and the fact that you have a sunny personality and show up on time won't be enough.

List your accomplishments. Demanding a pay raise is a bold move. Can you back it up? Be ready to tell your boss specifically how you've contributed to the bottom line. As a salesperson, have you moved more product than anyone else? As a project manager, have you delivered the goods on a major account? As a supervisor, have you cut costs in your department or gotten more than expected out of your employees? Think back over your successes, and write them down. Be specific: have numbers in place for total sales, percentage saved, revenue created. And be realistic. If your list is short, it's probably not the best time to ask for props.

Know what you're worth. Consider your skills, experience, and education, then find out what other people in similar positions and with similar backgrounds are making. For salary comparison, browse job listing ads on employment Web sites, visit salary survey portals like Salary.com, or talk to friends in the industry.[1] Then make a list. Your goal is to show that people with fewer qualifications than you are getting paid more. Often, a manager may be willing to adjust your salary once he has become better informed about the going rate.

Figure out what you want. Once you've done your research, you need to know how much of a raise you'd like to get. Would you be happy with a meager 3 percent cost-of-living raise to keep up with

---

1. Keep in mind that not all markets are equal. A $60,000 salary in San Francisco is not the same as a $60,000 salary in Birmingham, so make sure you adjust for your market.

inflation? Or do you want more? Once you've figured out what to ask for, increase that amount by another 2 percent or so.[2] This gives you some negotiating room. And remember: You don't just have to negotiate for a bigger paycheck. Better perks and benefits are sometimes as good as a raise. What if your boss offered more flexible hours, vacation days, or profit-sharing instead of an actual raise?

Know what's available. Be reasonable. How is your company doing? Is business good? Is performance up? Is there even room in the budget for a raise? Sometimes companies apply salary freezes in order to cut costs or ride out a bad economy, which usually means money is tight. And asking for a raise when your company is struggling is pretty bad form. *But* occasionally companies hold back some cash just in case promotional increases are needed. Ask around. Talk to human resources. Find out whether the budget can even handle the increase you're asking for.

TIMING IS CRITICAL

Use common sense. Your boss will be more willing to consider your request if you bring it up at the most opportune time, such as:

When you've just had a major success. Ask for a raise right after you've proven your value to the company. If you're coming off a major sale or the completion of a big project, there's no better time to ask.

After you've been given more responsibilities. Pay increases don't always accompany new positions or responsibility shifts. If your job has become more demanding but the change isn't reflected on your paycheck, then asking for more is a no-brainer.

When your boss is in a good mood. People who feel good are more likely to react positively to your request, especially if you're as valuable as you think you are. But the opposite also applies. If the

2. But only a couple percent. Don't be stupid and ask for something outrageous. That'll make your boss angry and make you look like a joke.

boss has had a bad day or a bad week, don't cap it off by making it worse. Either way, don't expect an immediate decision. Allow time for him or her to consider your request.

When your boss has time to talk. Managers are always busy, but don't poke your head into their office on Monday morning right after they show up for work, or on Friday afternoon when they're trying to wrap things up before the weekend.[3] Instead, make an appointment. That way you'll have plenty of time to present your case.

After you're mentally prepared. Think through your boss' potential objections. Practice your responses. Be ready to sell yourself and prove your value. And don't forget to anticipate how you'll respond if your boss says "no." The worst thing you can do is burst into tears or cop a bad attitude.

WHAT *NOT* TO DO

Above all, you want to go about the process of asking for a raise as professionally as possible. That means adhering to the following:

Don't whine about why you need the money. That's annoying. Seriously—everyone could use more money. Your boss doesn't care that you've got car payments due or a vacation to pay off. He or she only cares whether you're a valuable employee.

Don't compare yourself to other employees. Don't demand that your salary match that of the guy in the next cubicle. It's unprofessional to talk about your coworkers' salaries, and it's none of your business anyway. Compare your pay with the outside world, but not with anyone inside.

Don't get defensive or emotional. Act like a grownup. Stay positive. Whichever direction the conversation leads, don't let it upset you.

Don't be cocky. Confidence is good. It shows initiative. But

---

3. The best time to ask may be right after lunch, as pre-lunch hunger can make people irritable. Don't forget to pop in a breath mint and check your teeth for stray bits of lettuce.

overbearing arrogance? Not so good. If you go in there throwing down ultimatums, you'll immediately put your boss on the defensive. Spout out clichés like "If you don't give me a raise, then I'm gonna quit!" and he'll probably give you a chance to follow through on the threat.

FINAL WORDS

So, what if your boss flat-out denies your request for a raise? For one thing, you need to have a backup plan. Plan B should be a lower set of terms—a smaller raise, fewer benefits. Keep it positive and work down from there. If that gets turned down, then ask your boss for a suggestion. Add a little to it and see what happens.

If you're still out of luck, well, at least you've had the conversation. You've reminded your boss of your recent accomplishments. You probably impressed him or her with your boldness. You're in a good position to revisit the issue at your next performance review or the next time you score big. Go back to work, keep turning heads with your work ethic and success rate, and hopefully your boss will come around.

Good luck.

28

HOW TO TAKE A PHOTOGRAPH LIKE A PROFESSIONAL

When it comes to quickie point-and-shoot photography—the kind of digital or film snapshots you might take on a vacation or at a party—some people just take better photos than others. It's not a matter of equipment. In fact, owning the fanciest, most expensive digital camera in the world doesn't mean it'll result in great pictures. Why? Because a camera can't compose a photo by itself. It can't really light it either. That's your job, and composition and lighting are the keys to a nice photo. Here are a few tips to help you discover your inner Robert Doisneau.[1]

---

1. A popular and highly regarded twentieth-century French photographer, known for his charming Paris street scenes. Don't say the *Pocket Guide* ain't got no culture.

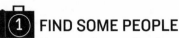 FIND SOME PEOPLE

Vacation photos of landscapes and rocks and beautiful mountain streams are pretty and everything (and Ansel Adams made a pretty good career out of the subject matter), but they're often much more fun to *take* than they are to look at. Seriously. To truly enjoy the beauty, you probably had to be there. One of the reasons this is true is because nature photos aren't always good at showing scale. We need a reference point, something that'll show us just how big that waterfall is.

The best reference point is also the best way to liven up a nature photo: Stick a person in there. Your friends or family. Innocent bystanders. Yourself, if you can figure out your camera's timer. Add some human interest, and make the beautiful nature stuff part of the background.

GET A LOT CLOSER

One of the most important things any photographer can do to improve his or her photographs is to take a step or two toward the subject. Zooming also helps. What you want to do is fill up the frame with your subject, especially if you're photographing a person. Move in. Crop it tight. The shots with the highest impact are the simple ones without extra clutter in the frame. They're more intimate and gobs more interesting.

Just don't get *too* close. Most cameras' closest focusing distance is about three feet. You can zoom all you want, but you can't stand any closer than that to your subject. Doing so will guarantee you a blurry mess. Check your manual for the precise physical distance your camera will allow.

③ ESCHEW THE MIDDLE

Or, in less pretentious wording, don't get all anal about making sure your shots are centered. Artsy folks are very into something called the "rule of thirds," which is a way to compose art and photography in order to achieve the most visual interest. The main idea? Unless you're going for a formal studio-style portrait, move your subject away from the middle of the picture.

Imagine your photo is a Tic-Tac-Toe grid, with two equally spaced horizontal lines and two vertical lines (dividing your photo into, yes, thirds). Then, place your subject—whether it's someone's face or a flower close-up or that Sasquatch you just spooked on your camping trip in the Pacific Northwest—at the intersection of one of those lines. Remember: Your auto-focus camera will focus on whatever is at the center of your viewfinder. To make sure you keep your off-centered subject sharp, you'll need to lock the focus by placing the subject in the middle, then recompose.[2]

④ STOP ALL THAT FLASHING

The automatic flash that's built into your camera is not nearly as cool as you think it is. Let's say you take a picture of some friends at a concert. They're just a few feet away from you. With an automatic flash, your friends will turn into pasty, shadowless albino freaks—washed out and overexposed against a completely dark and detail-free background.

You can get around that by turning off the automatic flash whenever possible. This is the little lightning bolt symbol on your camera, and what you want to do is push the button until there's a circle-with-a-line-through-it across that lightning bolt. This means your automatic camera will leave the shutter open long enough to

2. If you don't know, here's how to lock the focus. First, center your subject and press your picture-taking button (pros call this the shutter button) halfway down. You'll probably see a green light. This sets the focus distance to whatever is in the middle of the frame when the button was pushed. Then, while still pressing the button, recompose your shot to take the subject out of the center. Once you're happy with the composition, press the button the rest of the way down to actually take the picture.

get enough light for an exposure without the obnoxious flash.

Which leaves us a problem. The camera's longest shutter speed is likely around one second. Despite your above-average coolness and steady hand, you'll probably only be able to hold the camera perfectly still for one-thirtieth of a second. Result? The dreaded camera shake and a blurry photo. So you need to figure out a way to both hold the camera still and make the exposure faster. How?

Option 1: You can find more ambient light and move your subjects toward it. Have them open up their cell phones and shine the pleasing blue light on their faces. Something.

Option 2: Either put faster film in your camera (ISO 400 or 800, which require lots quicker exposures than ISO 100) or set your digital camera to a higher speed.

Option 3: Carry around a foldout tripod at all times. Or, if somehow that's not practical, find something to steady the camera against while you push the button. Another option: set the camera someplace stable (a rock, table, barstool, etc.) and set the self-timer. No button-pushing at all.

OKAY, YOU CAN FLASH OCCASIONALLY

The automatic devil flash on your camera isn't a complete waste. There will be times when you'll need to photograph someone outdoors who's in the shade, with a bright sunlit background behind her. (For instance, on a hotel balcony with a sunny beach in the background.) Your camera will expose for the sunny background, and the shady person will end up all dark and mysterious. But mostly dark.

This is when you use the flash—as fill light on the subject so she won't end up a blacked-out silhouette against a bright background. Your camera won't know to use the flash, though. For one thing, you should have turned it off by now, thanks to the above tip. And for another thing, the camera thinks everything is just fine because of the sunshine. Find your flash button again and press it until the solid lightning bolt shows back up.

You also need to know your flash's range. For most cameras, it's around fifteen feet. Anything past that is too far away to be lit up by the flash. You know those people who hold up their cameras at a concert to take a picture of the band fifty yards away? All that flash is doing is exposing the backs of the heads of the first fifteen feet of people in front of them. Flashes are useless for catching the action any farther away than that. So, back to Tip #2: Get A Lot Closer.

VARIETY

You've learned to take great photos. You know to get close to your subject and how to light it without spoiling things with a blinding flash. But if all of your photos are nice, glowing, rule-of-thirds close-ups of faces? People will lose interest. To keep your photo album from putting people to sleep, shake things up every once in a while.

Shoot a few vertical photos. Yes, you'll have to turn the camera sideways, but lots of things look so much better in vertical format. People, after all, are vertical. Whenever you want to emphasize height (a tree, a cliff, a basketball player), rotate the camera.

Change your point of view. Most photos work best at eye level, since this is normally how we look at the world. (Which means squatting down to photograph children.) But what if you dropped to a knee and shot upward from that low angle? It's a great way to show height or authority.[3] And shooting from a higher perspective often gives you more dramatic compositions.

Forget about posing and counting to three. Organized, "smile,

3. It's also a great way to emphasize someone's nostrils, so use this sparingly with people photos.

everyone" photos are nice because one of the great things about photography is recording that where-we-were-and-what-we-did moment. But some of the best photos are the candid ones, when the subject doesn't know he or she is being photographed. Sneaky photography is ideal for capturing realism and personality.

FINAL WORDS

A professional photographer with a $2,000 camera, a pack of $1,500 lenses, and a tripod is going to be able to do some cool things with his camera. But most of the beauty of his work will be in the framing and composition—what he chooses to shoot and how he chooses to shoot it. Guess what? You can do those things, too, without spending thousands of dollars. Get a decent point-and-shoot or digital camera, read your manual, and practice. Take lots of pictures, and you may just be the next Josef Koudelka.[4]

4. A Czech photographer known for his formal, documentary-style photography of the everyday rituals of gypsy communities.

CHAPTER TWENTY-NINE

REALLY HANDY INDEX OF BRIEF, PRACTICAL SUGGESTIONS

Nothing extraordinarily mind-blowing about this final chapter. Hopefully, you've already camped out on the really big stuff, and now you're much smarter than you used to be. Much more adult, too. Good job with that.

Let's close with a final look at a random selection of miscellaneous tips, tricks, and suggestions related to everyday life. All of them will make your life easier in some manner or fashion. And all of them are things you should know before you hit that nice round number looming on the horizon. Here they are, in order, from briefest to least brief.

☐ KEEP THE STANK OUTTA THE FRIDGE

Make sure your refrigerator maintains a pleasant smell by keeping an open box of baking soda inside it. Other odor-eating options include a can filled with charcoal, dried coffee grounds, or a cotton ball soaked in vanilla extract.

☐ DISRUPT THE ANT PARADE

If you've got a line of ants marching across your countertop, here's an effective and cheap way to get rid of them. Make a mixture of two-thirds cup water, one-third cup white vinegar, and two-to-three tablespoons of dish soap. Spray or paint it across the parade and watch the drama unfold.

☐ REDUCE STRESS AT WORK

The single best way to depressurize your workplace—other than hot tubs in the breakroom—is to keep your desk well organized. Try to straighten your desk at the end of every day and especially every Friday, so that you can start each day or week with a clean, soothing, inviting workspace.

☐ HIDE NICKS AND SCRATCHES

Unfortunately, it's really easy to scrape the white paint off your refrigerator, range oven, or any other major appliance. Cover these blemishes with high-quality typewriter correction fluid. Same goes for porcelain tiles and sinks. The fluid comes in multiple colors these days, so pick out one that matches, and no one will ever know.

☐ BRUSH YOUR WHEELS TO CLEANLINESS

Instead of spending big bucks on wheel polish for your aluminum or chrome car wheels, use plain old white toothpaste instead. You need fine abrasives to do the dirty work, and toothpaste has the perfect amount of said abrasive. Which is a major money saver. Apparently, if it's good enough for your teeth, it's good enough for car parts.[1]

☐ PIPE DOWN THAT DRIP

The quickest and easiest way to deal with a drippy faucet is to tie a piece of string (make it a couple of feet long, for good measure) around the faucet and into the drain. The annoying drips will quietly slide down the string without all the plop-plop-plopping that can drive you batty. Of course, this isn't a permanent solution— you'll still need to repair the leak—but it's a nice way to muffle the drip until you can get it fixed.

☐ UPDATE YOUR BATHROOM

Wanna change the look of your bathroom without dramatically changing the balance in your bank account? Unless there's a TLC program filming at your house, the best way to get a new look for a small amount of money is to buy new "softwares"—towels, rug(s), and shower curtain. Pick a new color scheme. Bring in contrasting but complementary colors. Or, for an even more drastic change, paint the walls with a bold, contemporary new color.

☐ KEEP CUT FLOWERS FRESH

Nothing's better than getting (or giving) fresh flowers. Nothing's more disappointing than watching them wilt. To keep them fresh for as long as possible, start by cutting the stem with a sharp, non-serrated knife. Make the cut in lukewarm water.[2] Cut at a slant to expose the most stem surface to the water, then remove any leaves that will be submerged. Fill the vase with, again, lukewarm water, then change the water every two days. Keeping the water fresh is,

---

1. Well, I've never even remotely come close to writing a sentence like *that* before.
2. This means the flowers actually get cut twice: once at the florist or from your garden, and then again when you get home. The reason for the second, underwater cut is to prevent a water-blocking air bubble from forming within the stem's water-sucking cells.

by far, the most important thing you can do to make flowers last longer. That, or leaving them in the garden in the first place.

☐ INCREASE YOUR CAR'S GAS MILEAGE

With gas prices seemingly always on the rise, there's no better time to maximize your mileage. Check your tires often, as under-inflated and badly aligned tires decrease your fuel efficiency. Avoid excessive idling. Observe speed limits (the faster you go, the worse your miles per gallon). Keep your windows closed at high speeds to reduce air drag. And be a mellow driver: Try to speed up gradually instead of punching the gas, and use cruise control whenever appropriate. One more tip: Don't use your trunk as a catchall storage device. All that extra weight means worse mileage. If it's not necessary, unpack it.

☐ REMEMBER A PERSON'S NAME

You're at a conference. One of your prized vendors introduces you to her boss. You pass by Mr. Bossman later that afternoon and say, "Hi! Good afternoon, uh … Mister, uh … hey, enjoying the conference?"

Congrats. You've just made yourself look stupid and have possibly annoyed a nice networking connection. Don't let it happen again.

The easiest way to commit someone's name to memory is through repetition. Once you hear their name via the introduction, repeat it back to them: "Very nice to meet you, Mr. Scutaro."[3] Then, ask a question about their name. *How do you spell your first name? Is that a family name? It sounds very exotic; does it come from another culture?* By changing their name into something more intimately associated to them, you've not only shown a genuine interest in the person, you've wrapped the info up amid several more brain connections.

---

3. Fun fact: You'll forget a person's name within ten seconds of meeting them unless you immediately repeat that name in conversation. At least, according to the research of some experts on the subject. I can't recall their names.

☐ PREPARE FOR A LOST PURSE OR WALLET

Unless you've recently gone all hardcore and adopted the wallet chain as a fashion accessory, there's always the possibility you could misplace that vital little package. Or have it stolen. It's way too easy to lose a purse or wallet, and in a time when identity theft is a significant threat, that's not a good thing. You'd need to act pretty quickly to cancel each of your credit, ATM, and debit cards before some sketchy villains start canceling out your bank account. But would you even know where to start?

Play it safe by cataloging each of the items you regularly carry in your purse or wallet. Empty it out, then start photocopying everything—credit cards, gas cards, driver's license, library cards, scraps of paper with cell phone numbers, you name it. If it lives in your wallet, make sure you keep a duplicate of it at home. And copy the front and back of each card. Obviously, the front is where you find the card number and expiration info. But the back is equally important because it lists the customer service number for reporting lost or stolen cards. Make copies, and keep those copies somewhere safe, secure, and easily accessible.

FINAL WORDS

This is the last chapter of the book, so be advised: We're not kidding around with this "final" thing. It's over. Done. So, good luck as you continue your journey toward adulthood, knowledge, and responsibility. May your life be one of wise financial decisions, healthy relationships, delicious smoothies, and nicely composed photography.

Have a great decade, and check back in a few years for *The Pocket Guide to Middle Age*.

[RELEVANTBOOKS]

FOR MORE INFORMATION
ABOUT OTHER RELEVANT BOOKS,
check out www.relevantbooks.com.